The Merchant
of Venice

D1319310

**A BLAISDELL BOOK
IN THE HUMANITIES**

EDITED BY
George Lyman Kittredge

Revised by Irving Ribner

William Shakespeare

The Merchant
of Venice

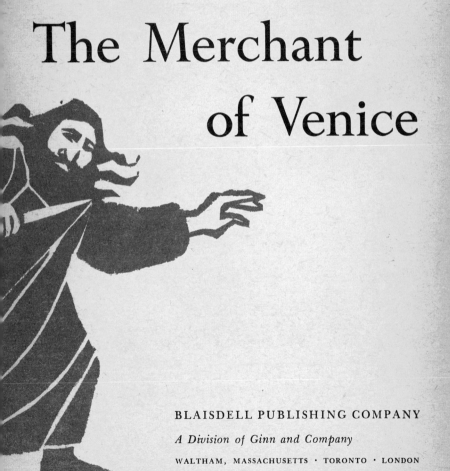

BLAISDELL PUBLISHING COMPANY

A Division of Ginn and Company

WALTHAM, MASSACHUSETTS · TORONTO · LONDON

PREFACE

The New Kittredge Shakespeares

The publication of George Lyman Kittredge's *Complete Works of Shakespeare* in 1936 was a landmark in Shakespeare scholarship. The teacher who for almost half a century had dominated and shaped the direction of Shakespearean study in America produced what was recognized widely as the finest edition of Shakespeare up to his time. In the preface to this edition Kittredge indicated his editorial principles; these allowed a paramount authority to the Folio of 1623 and countenanced few departures from it while, at the same time, refusing to "canonize the heedless type-setters of the Elizabethan printing house." Kittredge's work was marked by a judicious conservatism and a common sense rarely found in equal measure in earlier editors of Shakespeare. In the thirty-odd years which have gone by since the appearance of this monumental volume, however, considerable advances have been made in the establishment of Shakespeare's text, and our body of knowledge about the dates, sources, and general historical background of Shakespeare's plays has vastly increased. The present revision is designed to apply this new knowledge to Kittredge's work so that it may have as much value to the student and general reader of today as it had to those of thirty years ago.

Before his death Kittredge had issued, in addition to *The Complete Works,* separate editions of sixteen of the plays, each copiously annotated. Some of the notes were unusually elaborate, but they interpreted Shakespeare's language with a fullness and precision attained by few other commentators, for Kittredge had few equals in his intimate knowledge of Elizabethan English. In freshly annotating the plays I have, accordingly, tried to use

v

Kittredge's own notes as fully as space would permit. Where I have repeated his distinctive language or recorded his characteristic critical opinions, I have followed the note with the symbol [κ]; where Kittredge's definition of a term can be found in essentially the same words in other editions, I have not used the identifying symbol. Every annotator draws upon the full body of the notes of earlier editors, and to give credit for every note is impossible. Notes have been placed at page bottoms.

The brief introductions which Kittredge wrote for the plays have been replaced by new ones, for what seemed like indisputable fact some thirty years ago often appears today to be much more uncertain, and many new issues of which Kittredge was not aware have been raised in recent criticism. The new introductions seek to present what are now generally agreed to be basic facts about the plays and to give some indications of the directions which modern criticism has taken, although specific analyses of individual plays are avoided.

Such great authority attaches to Kittredge's text that it has not frequently — and never lightly — been departed from. Where changes have been made, they have usually involved the restoration of copy-text readings now generally accepted in place of the emendations of eighteenth- and nineteenth-century editors of which Kittredge, in spite of his extraordinary conservatism in this regard, sometimes too easily approved. Only rarely has an emendation been adopted in the present revision which was not also adopted by Kittredge. All departures from the copy-texts are indicated in the notes, emendations followed by the names of the editors by whom they were first proposed. Wherever Kittredge's text has been departed from for any reason, his reading is given in the notes. Modern spelling has in a few instances been substituted for Elizabethan forms which are mere spelling variations but which Kittredge nevertheless retained. His punctuation has not been altered except in a few very rare instances.

The system of recording elisions and contractions which Kittredge explained in his introduction to *The Complete Works* has been retained, as has his method of preserving to the fullest the copy-text stage directions, with all additions to them enclosed within square brackets. Although modern editors recognize the

vagueness of the place settings of Elizabethan plays and are re-
luctant to include the place designations so favoured by eight-
eenth- and nineteenth-century editors, much historical interest
nevertheless attaches to these, and Kittredge's place designations
accordingly have been retained between square brackets. Kittredge's attempt to retain the line numbering of the Globe text,
which resulted in considerable irregularity in prose passages, has
been abandoned, and the lines of each play have been freshly
numbered. Kittredge's act and scene divisions have been retained,
as has his practice of surrounding by square brackets those divisions which are not in the copy-texts.

The plan of *The New Kittredge Shakespeares* is a comprehensive one. They will include a new edition of *The Complete
Works* and individual editions of each of the plays, the sonnets,
and the poems. A comprehensive introduction to Shakespeare's
life, times, and theatrical milieu will be published both as a separate volume and as an introduction to *The Complete Works*.

IRVING RIBNER

INTRODUCTION

The Merchant of Venice

◇◇◇◇◇
◇◇◇◇◇ On July 22, 1598, the printer James Roberts entered in
◇◇◇◇◇ the Stationers' Register "a booke of the Merchant of
Venyce or otherwise called the Iewe of Venyce." In 1600 Roberts
transferred his rights in the play to Thomas Heyes and printed
the play for Heyes in a quarto (Q^1) issued in that same year. It
is a good text, probably printed from Shakespeare's own manu-
script, although it does have considerable confusion in the speech
headings between the names Salerio and Salarino, and it is without act or scene division. It served as the basis for a second quarto
printed by William Jaggard for Thomas Pavier in 1619 (Q^2),
although fraudulently dated 1600, and for the text in the Folio
of 1623 (F^1), where act divisions, but no scene divisions, have
been added. The present edition is based upon Q^1 except where
there is clear evidence of error. Speech headings have been regu-
larized, with the name Salarino eliminated entirely and Salerio
used uniformly in its place.

DATE

The Merchant of Venice must have been written before its entry in the Stationers' Register in the summer of 1598, and it must
have been performed long enough to have acquired some reputation before the entry in the Stationers' Register on September 7,
1598, of Francis Meres' Palladis Tamia, in which the play is
praised. To date the play more precisely is difficult. Some scholars
have held that, at least in its earliest form, it must have been
written in 1594. This argument has rested largely on the assumption that there is an allusion at IV.i.133-7 to the execution on

June 7, 1594, of the Portuguese Jew Roderigo Lopez for his supposed part in a conspiracy to poison Queen Elizabeth and the Portuguese pretender, Don Antonio. The Lopez affair seems to have set off a wave of anti-Semitism in London, during which Marlowe's *Jew of Malta* was revived for fifteen performances, and it has been held that Shakespeare wrote his play to capitalize upon this interest.

That the lines in question do refer to Lopez, however, is extremely doubtful. Wolves were actually hanged for human slaughter in Shakespeare's day — as were dogs for attacking sheep — and that a theatre audience would translate *wolf* into the Latin *lupus* and thus make a connection with Lopez is as unlikely as is the assumption that Shakespeare was one to capitalize on a wave of anti-Semitism. Other topical allusions that have been detected in the play are equally dubious, although the most impressive of them is the probable allusion at I.i.27 to the St. Andrew, a Spanish ship captured at Cadiz in 1596 and because of its size continually in danger of foundering as it was brought back to England. The capture was very much a subject of interest and discussion. That the play was written sometime between 1596 and 1598 is a conclusion that accords well with its obvious maturity of style.

SOURCES

Shakespeare's play involves a skillful combination of several romantic stories, each of ancient origin and extant in many versions. In the first story of the fourth day of the *Il Pecorone* of Ser Giovanni Fiorentino, a collection of *novelle* written at the end of the fourteenth century but not printed in Italian until 1588 and never translated into English in Shakespeare's time, three of the elements of Shakespeare's play may be found already combined: the wooing of the lady of Belmont, the pledge of a pound of flesh as surety for debt, and the episode of the rings. In this version the lover who would win the lady of Belmont must stay awake with her all night, but is twice prevented from doing so by a sleeping potion, which on the third try he is able to avoid. For this love test Shakespeare substituted that of the

three caskets, an ancient parable of oriental origins found in many forms, but for which Shakespeare seems to have used the version in Richard Robinson's 1577 translation of the *Gesta Romanorum*. The elopement of Jessica, the final major element in the play, has often been attributed to the example of Marlowe's Abigail in *The Jew of Malta*, but the Jew's fair daughter and her Christian lover are conventional motifs of medieval story to be found in many places, and Shakespeare's episode is not so close to Marlowe's as to make dependence certain. That Shakespeare knew Marlowe's play and took some suggestions from it, particularly the throwing down of the money bags, is likely, but the influence of *The Jew of Malta* on *The Merchant of Venice* has generally been overestimated. The elopement of Jessica is much closer, in fact, to the fourteenth story of the *Novellino* of Massuccio of Salerno, another collection of fifteenth-century novelle which like *Il Pecorone* was unavailable to Shakespeare other than in the Italian. Shakespeare may have taken some suggestions also from Anthony Munday's prose novel, *Zelauto or the Fountain of Fame*, another bond story involving a daughter, although here the usurer is a Christian rather than a Jew.

AN EARLIER PLAY

There is some reason to suspect that Shakespeare may have found the casket story already combined with the elements in *Il Pecorone* in some earlier play now lost, and thus have had no need for recourse to the Italian. Stephen Gosson, writing in *The Schools of Abuse* (1578), took occasion to exempt two plays from his general condemnation of the drama: "The *Iew* and *Ptolome*, Showne at the Bull, the one representing the gredinesse of worldly chusers, and bloody mindes of Usurers. . . ." The bond story of Shakespeare's play has been equated by some critics with the "bloody mindes of Usurers" and the casket story with "the greediness of worldly chusers," and this lost play is considered to have been Shakespeare's primary source. This could have been the case, but it is far from proven, the assumption upon which it rests being merely uncertain conjectures. The truth is that we know absolutely nothing about the play to which Gossen referred.

Plays in which Jews figure as principal characters, it should be noted, are extremely rare upon the Elizabethan stage. Earlier than Shakespeare we have only Marlowe's *Jew of Malta* and Robert Wilson's *The Three Ladies of London* (1584), a late morality play in which a Jew named Gerontus teaches an errant Christian merchant the evils of his ways by an act of kindness. To find Jews in drama beyond this we must go to the crude fifteenth-century *Croxton Play of the Sacrament* and to the Jews of the Corpus Christi Day cycles. A *Jew of Venice* by Thomas Dekker was entered in the Stationers' Register on September 9, 1653, but of this lost play nothing whatsoever is known. It may have been written in imitation of Shakespeare's. It is thus not entirely accurate to speak, as some have done, of the Jew as a traditional stage stereotype in Shakespeare's time.

THE BOND STORY

Stories involving the forfeiting of human flesh appear in various forms in ancient religious tales of India and Persia. The Twelve Tables of Roman Law actually permitted creditors to claim the flesh of their debtors as a last resort, and stories naturally grew out of this practice. The tale of the wicked usurer denied his pound of flesh by a lawyer's clever distinction between flesh and blood came to have wide currency in medieval Europe. In early versions, such as the one in the *Gesta Romanorum,* the usurer is not a Jew, and he is not a Jew even in such later versions as the one in Anthony Munday's *Zelauto.* Gradually, however, the usurer came to be identified as a Jew, as he is for the first time in the thirteenth-century *Cursor Mundi* version of the tale. The story was shaped as one of a large body of medieval anti-Semitic legends in which a Jew attempts to kill a Christian — often to get human flesh to eat at the feast of the Passover, as primitive fear and superstition led some medieval Christians to believe — but is frustrated in his attempt, usually by some miraculous intervention, and at last converted to Christianity. Among such legends belongs the one in Chaucer's "Prioress' Tale." The story took such a form in *Il Pecorone* and in various Elizabethan versions, including *The Ballad of Gernutus,* which is probably pre-Shakespearean, and the one in *The Orator,* translated in 1596 by L.P. (Lazarus Piot) from the French of Alexandre Sylvain. That Shakespeare may have known these Elizabethan versions is possible.

SHYLOCK

Although Shakespeare's Shylock is the villain of the play, he is not the kind of villain represented by his prototypes in medieval story. The Jews of medieval anti-Semitic legend needed no motivation beyond the fact that they were Jews eager for Christian flesh. Shakespeare humanizes Shylock. There is some evidence of revision in the play, which would indicate that what in an earlier version may have been merely the traditional medieval stereotype has been developed by Shakespeare into a character whose sense of injury is fed by the elopement of his daughter and who seeks revenge for injuries just as a Christian might seek it. This is most evident in III.1. In lines 37–43 Shylock, lamenting his daughter's flight, shows that he is aware of Antonio's losses at sea, sees the bond as "another bad match," and vows revenge. Yet at line 89ff. he appears to hear the news of Antonio's misfortune from Tubal for the first time and then goes into an ecstacy of joy at the prospect of gaining his pound of flesh. This second reaction to the news seems to represent a more primitive conception of Shylock than the first and may well represent the survival of an earlier form of the play. That Shylock is humanized by Shakespeare does not make him less of a villain. It is merely that his villainy is explained in credible human terms and not as part of an absurd racial myth. Thus although Shakespeare's play is anti-Semitic — it could scarce have been otherwise in his time — it is not so anti-Semitic as it might have been.

JEWS IN SHAKESPEARE'S LONDON

Although Jews were officially expelled from England by King Edward I and officially welcomed back by Oliver Cromwell, we know that there were Jews living in Shakespeare's London. A good account of them may be found in C. J. Sisson's "A Colony of Jews in Shakespeare's England," *Essays and Studies, XXIII*

(1938), 38–51. Although they outwardly professed Christianity and attended Church of England services as the law prescribed, they also carried on their Jewish religious rites and maintained their identity as Jews. Whether or not Shakespeare himself ever knew any Jews we shall never know, and the matter is of no pertinence to the play, for to suppose that Shylock is based upon an actual person is absurd. It is important to our understanding of *The Merchant of Venice* to recognize, however, that whereas usury was one of the most vital problems of Shakespeare's age, anti-Semitism was neither an issue nor a problem in his day. Of the actual Jews in Shakespeare's London, Sisson has written the following:

> Full toleration certainly was not yet achieved. But the Jews in London had the immense comfort of communal life, undisturbed, with full freedom to carry on their trades and professions, and even the further solace of the regular practice of religious rites in the home, even if in secret. The Jewish problem was, in truth, no problem in the reign of Elizabeth. The Jews that London knew, and that Shakespeare might have met, were not Shylocks.

THE CASKETS AND THE RINGS

The casket story was originally a parable illustrating the perversity of a judgment that preferred outward show to true substance. In this form it appears in the story of *Barlaam and Joasaph,* written in Greek in the ninth century by Joannes Damascenus and translated into Latin sometime before the thirteenth century. In various forms it appears in the *Speculum Historiale* (*XV*, 10) of Vincent of Beauvais, in the *Legenda Aurea* (Cap. 176) of Jacobus de Voragine, in Boccaccio's *Decameron* (First story, tenth day), in John Gower's *Confessio Amantis* (*V*, 2273–2434), and in Robinson's version of the *Gesta Romanorum,* which was probably Shakespeare's source although all the other versions were available to him. In *The Merchant of Venice* this ancient device is used to explain the nature of true love — the principal theme of the play — and Shakespeare here relies upon the threefold definition of love that goes back to Plato. Morocco chooses love of the senses, Arragon love of the intellect, and Bassanio passes the test by choosing love of the understanding, the highest kind of love, which is an intuitive union of mind in which the lover gives all without expectation of gain.

The relation of the love of man for woman to the friendship between man and man is a common Renaissance theme. It is a subject of Shakespeare's sonnets, and it is explored in the story of the rings. It was believed that man could not truly love woman unless he could love his friend. Friendship between men was considered to be on a higher intellectual plane than love between man and woman. Bassanio acknowledges this principle when he gives his ring to the disguised Portia as payment for the life of his friend, thinking that in doing so he is giving up the love of his wife for which the ring stands. Portia, in forgiving him, recognizes that it is proper that he do so; were he not willing to sacrifice all, including his wife, for his friend, he would be incapable of truly loving her. Through the course of the play Bassanio, who begins as somewhat of a careless adventurer, learns the meaning of true friendship as well as true love.

JUSTICE VERSUS MERCY

The nature of love is Shakespeare's central theme in *The Merchant of Venice,* and all of the diverse elements of the play are combined to serve this theme. The love of man for woman and of man for his friend are conceived of in terms of Renaissance neo-Platonism as emanations on the earthly plane of the supreme love of God for man, and this divine love is expressed in mercy. By this consideration the story of Shylock and his bond is linked to the stories of the caskets and the rings. The court scene involves a contest between mercy and justice. The argument for mercy depends upon the Christian doctrine of original sin: if justice only were to be observed in heaven, all men would be damned; only through God's mercy can man hope for salvation in spite of original sin, and if he would hope for the mercy of God in heaven, he must himself extend mercy to his fellow men on earth. Shylock's argument is based upon what was (in a great oversimplification) conceived to be the Old Testament position: that man would be judged in heaven by a strict code of justice and rewarded or punished according to his deeds on earth.

Portia's position is triumphant. She is able to defeat the claims of justice by a strict observance of justice itself, and when the argument for justice has been defeated, Shylock himself is shown mercy rather than the justice he had demanded. His money will go to his daughter and her husband, as it should, because they are his only heirs, and by his conversion to Christianity the salvation of his soul will be made possible. The conversion of Shylock is an important element in *The Merchant of Venice,* just as conversion figured in medieval anti-Semitic legendry. The elopement of Jessica repeats a traditional motif — the sympathetically treated Jew's daughter who wins salvation through the love of a Christian — and it helps prepare the audience for the conversion of her father. *The Merchant of Venice* ends appropriately in the magic world of Belmont in a final act of peace and tranquility, the harmony of earth being echoed by the music of the spheres, in which all of the problems of the play have been resolved.

The Merchant
of Venice

[DRAMATIS PERSONÆ.

THE DUKE OF VENICE.
THE PRINCE OF MOROCCO, } *suitors to* PORTIA.
THE PRINCE OF ARRAGON,
ANTONIO, *A Venetian merchant.*
BASSANIO, *his friend, suitor to* PORTIA.
SOLANIO,
SALERIO, } *friends to* ANTONIO *and* BASSANIO.
GRATIANO,
LORENZO, *in love with* JESSICA.
SHYLOCK, *a Jew.*
TUBAL, *a Jew, his friend.*
LAUNCELOT GOBBO, *a clown, servant to* SHYLOCK.
OLD GOBBO, *father to* LAUNCELOT.
LEONARDO, *servant to* BASSANIO.
BALTHASAR, } *servants to* PORTIA.
STEPHANO,

PORTIA, *an heiress.*
NERISSA, *her waiting gentlewoman.*
JESSICA, *daughter to* SHYLOCK.

Magnificoes, Officers, Jailer, Servants, and other Attendants.

SCENE. — *Partly at Venice and partly at Belmont, Portia's estate.*]

Act One

◇◇◇

[SCENE I. *Venice. A street.*]

Enter Antonio, Salerio, *and* Solanio.

ANT. In sooth, I know not why I am so sad.
  It wearies me; you say it wearies you;
  But how I caught it, found it, or came by it,
  What stuff 'tis made of, whereof it is born,
  I am to learn;   5
  And such a want-wit sadness makes of me
  That I have much ado to know myself.

SALER. Your mind is tossing on the ocean;
  There where your argosies with portly sail —
  Like signiors and rich burghers on the flood, 10
  Or, as it were, the pageants of the sea —
  Do overpeer the petty traffickers,
  That cursy to them, do them reverence,
  As they fly by them with their woven wings.

SOLAN. Believe me, sir, had I such venture forth, 15

I.i. 1 *In . . . sad* The reasons for Antonio's initial melancholy have been much debated. As we can tell from line 119, Antonio already knows that his friend will be leaving in quest of a lady, and this fact may explain his sadness. Perhaps Shakespeare is merely setting a tone which will foreshadow Antonio's later troubles. 5 *am to* have yet to. 9 *argosies* merchant ships. *portly* swollen (with wind). 11 *pageants* elaborately decorated floats drawn through the streets as parts of public shows or pageants; sometimes they were drawn along the Thames river. 12 *overpeer* look down on. 13 *cursy* bow (a variant of "curtsy"). The metaphor is suggested by the lesser vessels (petty traffickers) bobbing up and down in the wake of the large argosy. 14 *woven wings* sails. 15 *venture* commercial enterprise, investment.

I

The better part of my affections would
Be with my hopes abroad. I should be still
Plucking the grass to know where sits the wind,
Piring in maps for ports, and piers, and roads;
And every object that might make me fear   20
Misfortune to my ventures, out of doubt
Would make me sad.

SALER.   My wind, cooling my broth,
Would blow me to an ague when I thought
What harm a wind too great might do at sea.
I should not see the sandy hourglass run   25
But I should think of shallows and of flats,
And see my wealthy Andrew dock'd in sand,
Vailing her high top lower than her ribs
To kiss her burial. Should I go to church
And see the holy edifice of stone   30
And not bethink me straight of dangerous rocks,
Which, touching but my gentle vessel's side,
Would scatter all her spices on the stream,
Enrobe the roaring waters with my silks,
And, in a word, but even now worth this,   35
And now worth nothing? Shall I have the thought
To think on this, and shall I lack the thought
That such a thing bechanc'd would make me sad?
But tell not me! I know Antonio
Is sad to think upon his merchandise.   40

ANT.   Believe me, no. I thank my fortune for it,
My ventures are not in one bottom trusted,
Nor to one place; nor is my whole estate
Upon the fortune of this present year.

---

17 *still* continually.   19 *Piring* peering and prying (Q¹; Q²: "piering").   *roads*
anchorages.   23 *ague* fit of trembling fear [K].   26 *flats* sand bars.   27 *Andrew*
the name of a ship. A Spanish galleon captured at Cadiz in 1596 and brought to
England was, in fact, named the "St. Andrew."   *dock'd* ROWE; Q¹: "docks."   28
Vailing lowering.   35–6 *but even . . . nothing* at one moment I may have so
much wealth and at the next moment nothing.   36 *thought* ability to think.   37
on of, about.   38 *bechanc'd* if it should happen.   42 *bottom* ship (specifically,
the hold).   50 *Janus* the Roman god of doors and entrances, who had two faces,

Therefore my merchandise makes me not sad.   45

SOLAN.   Why, then you are in love.

ANT.   Fie, fie!

SOLAN.   Not in love neither? Then let us say you are sad
Because you are not merry; and 'twere as easy
For you to laugh, and leap, and say you are merry
Because you are not sad. Now, by two-headed Janus,   50
Nature hath fram'd strange fellows in her time:
Some that will evermore peep through their eyes,
And laugh like parrots at a bagpiper;
And other of such vinegar aspect
That they'll not show their teeth in way of smile,   55
Though Nestor swear the jest be laughable.

Enter Bassanio, Lorenzo, *and* Gratiano.

Here comes Bassanio, your most noble kinsman,
Gratiano, and Lorenzo. Fare ye well.
We leave you now with better company.

SALER.   I would have stay'd till I had made you merry,   60
If worthier friends had not prevented me.

ANT.   Your worth is very dear in my regard.
I take it your own business calls on you,
And you embrace th' occasion to depart.

SALER.   Good morrow, my good lords.   65

BASS.   Good signiors both, when shall we laugh? Say, when?
You grow exceeding strange. Must it be so?

one smiling and the other frowning.   52 *peep . . . eyes* look with their eyes half-
closed when they affect laughter [K].   53 *laugh . . . bagpiper* laugh without
cause, as the foolish parrot will laugh at the melancholy sound of a bagpipe.   54
vinegar aspect sour demeanour.   56 *Nestor* the aged councillor of the Greeks in
the Trojan war, a symbol of gravity who would not easily be moved to laughter.
61 *prevented* forestalled.   66 *laugh* have a merry meeting.   67 *strange* unfriendly
(a polite exaggeration).

SALER.   We'll make our leisures to attend on yours.

Exeunt Salerio *and* Solanio.

LOR.   My Lord Bassanio, since you have found Antonio,
We two will leave you; but at dinner time   70
I pray you have in mind where we must meet.

BASS.   I will not fail you.

GRA.   You look not well, Signior Antonio.
You have too much respect upon the world;
They lose it that do buy it with much care.   75
Believe me, you are marvellously chang'd.

ANT.   I hold the world but as the world, Gratiano —
A stage, where every man must play a part,
And mine a sad one.

GRA.   Let me play the fool.
With mirth and laughter let old wrinkles come,   80
And let my liver rather heat with wine
Than my heart cool with mortifying groans.
Why should a man whose blood is warm within
Sit like his grandsire cut in alablaster?
Sleep when he wakes? and creep into the jaundice   85
By being peevish? I tell thee what, Antonio —
I love thee, and it is my love that speaks —
There are a sort of men whose visages
Do cream and mantle like a standing pond,
And do a wilful stillness entertain   90
With purpose to be dress'd in an opinion

---

68 *We'll make . . . yours* whenever you are at leisure we will contrive to be at
leisure also in order to meet you and enjoy your society [K].   74 *respect upon*
regard for. *world* worldly prosperity.   75 *They lose . . . care* one who is too
anxious for worldly prosperity may wear himself out and so die and leave the
world altogether [K].   76 *marvellously* exceedingly.   81 *liver . . . wine* Drinking
was believed to heat the liver, source of the passions.   82 *heart . . . groans*
Sighs and groans were believed to draw blood away from the heart.   *mortifying*
deadening.   84 *Sit . . . alablaster* Tombs in English churches were often adorned
with monuments of the dead made of alablaster (an old form of "alabaster").   85
Sleep . . . wakes be so dumpish even in his waking hours that he may be said to
be asleep [K].   85 *jaundice* a medical disorder believed to cause depression.   88
sort considerable number.   89 *cream and mantle* become covered with a mantle
of scum — a strong expression for the sallow coating of melancholy which over-

Of wisdom, gravity, profound conceit;
As who should say, "I am Sir Oracle,
And when I ope my lips, let no dog bark!"
O my Antonio, I do know of these   95
That therefore only are reputed wise
For saying nothing; when, I am very sure,
If they should speak, would almost dam those ears
Which, hearing them, would call their brothers fools.
I'll tell thee more of this another time.   100
But fish not with this melancholy bait
For this fool gudgeon, this opinion.
Come, good Lorenzo. Fare ye well awhile.
I'll end my exhortation after dinner.

LOR.   Well, we will leave you then till dinner time.   105
I must be one of these same dumb wise men,
For Gratiano never lets me speak.

GRA.   Well, keep me company but two years moe,
Thou shalt not know the sound of thine own tongue.

ANT.   Fare you well. I'll grow a talker for this gear.   110

GRA.   Thanks, i' faith; for silence is only commendable
In a neat's tongue dried and a maid not vendible.

                 Exeunt [Gratiano *and* Lorenzo].

ANT.   Is that anything now?

BASS.   Gratiano speaks an infinite deal of nothing, more than
any man in all Venice. His reasons are as two grains of 115

---

spreads a man's face when in the dumps [K].   *standing* stagnant.   90 *wilfull still-*
ness entertain assume an obstinate silence.   91 *opinion* reputation.   92 *conceit*
power of thought.   98 *would* they would.   98–9 *dam . . . fools* (a) cause their
hearers to stop up their ears against the foolishness they are hearing (b) cause
their hearers to call them fools and thus incur damnation for insulting their
brothers. Cf. MATTHEW, v, 22: "but whosoever shall say, Thou fool, shall be in
danger of hell fire." *dam* Q¹, Q², F¹; F⁴, K: "damn."   101–2 *fish not . . . opinion*
do not use melancholy to gain a reputation based upon foolish public opinion.
gudgeon a proverbially foolish fish used as bait. To "swallow a gudgeon" is to
be taken in by a falsehood.   108 *moe* more.   110 *for this gear* because of the
"stuff" you have just uttered.   112 *neat's tongue* ox tongue, usually stuffed with
cloves to render it more dry and thus supposedly more wholesome.   112 *vendible*
salable, i.e. marriageable.   115 *reasons* intelligent statements.

wheat hid in two bushels of chaff. You shall seek all day
ere you find them; and when you have them, they are
not worth the search.

ANT.   Well, tell me now, what lady is the same
To whom you swore a secret pilgrimage   120
That you to-day promis'd to tell me of?

BASS.   'Tis not unknown to you, Antonio,
How much I have disabled mine estate
By something showing a more swelling port
Than my faint means would grant continuance;   125
Nor do I now make moan to be abridg'd
From such a noble rate; but my chief care
Is to come fairly off from the great debts
Wherein my time, something too prodigal,
Hath left me gag'd. To you, Antonio,   130
I owe the most, in money and in love;
And from your love I have a warranty
To unburden all my plots and purposes
How to get clear of all the debts I owe.

ANT.   I pray you, good Bassanio, let me know it;   135
And if it stand, as you yourself still do,
Within the eye of honour, be assur'd
My purse, my person, my extremest means
Lie all unlock'd to your occasions.

BASS.   In my schooldays, when I had lost one shaft,   140
I shot his fellow of the selfsame flight
The selfsame way with more advised watch,
To find the other forth; and by adventuring both

---

123 *disabled mine estate* squandered my fortune.   124 *something* somewhat.
swelling port extravagant way of living.   125 *grant continuance* enable me to
continue in.   126 *to be abridg'd* about being cut off (from my extravagant way
of life).   127 *rate* style of living.   129 *time* youth.   130 *gag'd* engaged, in debt.
136–7 *if it stand . . . honour* if it comes within the limits of what will be recognized as honour when one looks at it [K].   139 *occasions* requirements.   141
fellow . . . flight another arrow of equal size and weight, calculated to fly as
far as the other.   142 *advised* careful.   143 *forth* out.   *adventuring* risking.   144
urge . . . proof offer this experience from my childhood.   145 *pure innocence*
(a) childlike sincerity (b) foolishness.   146 *wilful* self-willed, spoiled.   148 *self*
same.   150 *or* either.   151 *hazard* speculation, risk.   154 *wind . . . circum-*

I oft found both. I urge this childhood proof
Because what follows is pure innocence.   145
I owe you much, and, like a wilful youth,
That which I owe is lost; but if you please
To shoot another arrow that self way
Which you did shoot the first, I do not doubt,
As I will watch the aim, or to find both,   150
Or bring your latter hazard back again
And thankfully rest debtor for the first.

ANT.   You know me well, and herein spend but time
To wind about my love with circumstance;
And out of doubt you do me now more wrong   155
In making question of my uttermost
Than if you had made waste of all I have.
Then do but say to me what I should do
That in your knowledge may by me be done,
And I am prest unto it. Therefore speak.   160

BASS.   In Belmont is a lady richly left;
And she is fair, and, fairer than that word,
Of wondrous virtues. Sometimes from her eyes
I did receive fair speechless messages.
Her name is Portia — nothing undervalu'd   165
To Cato's daughter, Brutus' Portia.
Nor is the wide world ignorant of her worth;
For the four winds blow in from every coast
Renowned suitors, and her sunny locks
Hang on her temples like a golden fleece,   170
Which makes her seat of Belmont Colchos' strond,
And many Jasons come in quest of her.

---

stance wrap with ceremonious talk a request which you might make to me directly
because I love you [K].   155 *out of doubt* beyond question.   156 *making* . . .
uttermost doubting that I will do my utmost to serve you [K].   160 *prest* prepared.
161 *richly left* left rich (by her father's will).   162 *fairer . . . word* fairer than
the word "fair" can describe.   163–4 *Sometimes . . . messages* This passage in-
dicates clearly that Bassanio is genuinely in love with Portia, although the nature
of his request to Antonio makes it appropriate that he should emphasize particularly the worldly advantage to be derived from marrying the heiress [K].   171
seat residence.   *Colchos' strond* the shore of Colchos, land of the Golden
Fleece sought and won by Jason.

O my Antonio, had I but the means
To hold a rival place with one of them,
I have a mind presages me such thrift   175
That I should questionless be fortunate!

ANT. Thou know'st that all my fortunes are at sea;
.Neither have I money, nor commodity
To raise a present sum. Therefore go forth;
Try what my credit can in Venice do.   180
That shall be rack'd, even to the uttermost,
To furnish thee to Belmont to fair Portia.
Go presently inquire, and so will I,
Where money is; and I no question make
To have it of my trust, or for my sake.   *Exeunt.* 185

✦✦✦✦✦✦✦✦✦✦✦✦✦

[SCENE II. *Belmont.* Portia's *house.*]

Enter Portia *with her waiting woman,* Nerissa.

POR. By my troth, Nerissa, my little body is aweary of this
great world.

NER. You would be, sweet madam, if your miseries were in
the same abundance as your good fortunes are; and yet,
for aught I see, they are as sick that surfeit with too   5
much as they that starve with nothing. It is no mean
happiness, therefore, to be seated in the mean. Super-

---

174 *rival place* place as a rival.   175 *thrift* (a) profit (b) good fortune.   178
commòdity merchandise.   181 *rack'd* stretched out.   183 *presently* instantly.
185 *of my trust . . . sake* on account of the confidence people have in me or else
for the sake of friendship [K].
   I.II. 1 *troth* faith.   5 *surfeit* overeat.   7 *seated in the mean* have neither too
much nor to little, the golden mean.   7–8 *Superfluity . . . hairs* excessive wealth
causes one to age (get white hairs) the sooner.   8 *competency* modest means.   10
sentences moral maxims.   13 *chapels . . . churches* poor chapels would have to
be enlarged into churches to hold the worshippers who would throng thither.
13–14 *poor men's . . . princes* many a poor man might have become a prince,

fluity comes sooner by white hairs, but competency lives longer.

POR.   Good sentences, and well pronounc'd.   10

NER.   They would be better if well followed.

POR.   If to do were as easy as to know what were good to do, chapels had been churches, and poor men's cottages princes' palaces. It is a good divine that follows his own instructions. I can easier teach twenty what were good   15 to be done than be one of the twenty to follow mine own teaching. The brain may devise laws for the blood, but a hot temper leaps o'er a cold decree: such a hare is madness the youth, to skip o'er the meshes of good counsel the cripple. But this reasoning is not in the   20 fashion to choose me a husband. O me, the word "choose"! I may neither choose who I would nor refuse who I dislike, so is the will of a living daughter curb'd by the will of a dead father. Is it not hard, Nerissa, that I cannot choose one nor refuse none?   25

NER.   Your father was ever virtuous; and holy men at their death have good inspirations. Therefore the lott'ry that he hath devised in these three chests of gold, silver, and lead, whereof who chooses his meaning chooses you, will no doubt never be chosen by any rightly but one who   30 you shall rightly love. But what warmth is there in your affection towards any of these princely suitors that are already come?

POR.   I pray thee overname them; and as thou namest them, I will describe them; and according to my description   35 level at my affection.

since a poor man's knowledge of what to do is better than any prince's actions [K].   14 *divine* preacher.   16 *than be one* F¹; Q¹: "then to be one."   17 *blood* passions.   18 *temper* temperament.   *cold* calm and considerate.   19 *skip o'er the meshes* the meshes of the net by means of which good counsel would restrain him. The figure is of course from the netting of hares [K].   20-1 *not in . . . husband* not of the kind which will advance me toward a solution of the question how I am to choose a husband [K].   29 *his meaning* that one which your father intended should be selected.   30-1 *one who . . . love* one who will love you in the proper manner.   32 *affection* feelings.   36 *level at my affection* aim or guess at how I feel towards them.

NER.   First, there is the Neapolitan prince.

POR.   Ay, that's a colt indeed, for he doth nothing but talk
        of his horse; and he makes it a great appropriation to
        his own good parts that he can shoe him himself. I am   40
        much afeard my lady his mother play'd false with a
        smith.

NER.   Then is there the County Palatine.

POR.   He doth nothing but frown; as who should say, "An
        you will not have me, choose!" He hears merry tales and   45
        smiles not. I fear he will prove the weeping philosopher
        when he grows old, being so full of unmannerly sadness
        in his youth. I had rather be married to a death's-head
        with a bone in his mouth than to either of these. God
        defend me from these two!   50

NER.   How say you by the French lord, Monsieur Le Bon?

POR.   God made him, and therefore let him pass for a man.
        In truth, I know it is a sin to be a mocker; but he —
        why, he hath a horse better than the Neapolitan's, a
        better bad habit of frowning than the Count Palatine.   55
        He is every man in no man. If a throstle sing, he falls
        straight a-cap'ring; he will fence with his own shadow.
        If I should marry him, I should marry twenty husbands.
        If he would despise me, I would forgive him; for if he
        love me to madness, I shall never requite him.   60

NER.   What say you then to Falconbridge, the young baron of
        England?

POR.   You know I say nothing to him; for he understands not
        me, nor I him. He hath neither Latin, French, nor
        Italian; and you will come into the court and swear   65

---

38 *colt* young fool.   39–40 *he makes . . . parts* he regards it as something which
adds much to his own accomplishments [K].   43 *Then* Q²; Q¹: "than."   46 *weep-
ing philosopher* Heraclitus.   48 *death's head* skull.   56 *throstle* thrush (POPE;
Q¹: "Trassell").   57 *a-cap'ring* dancing; i.e. he will dance no matter who calls
the tune.   58 *twenty husbands* because he is so volatile, being many men in one.
64–5 *He hath . . . Italian* The disinclination of the English to learn any foreign
language fluently was and is proverbial [K].   67 *proper* handsome. *picture* mere
appearance.   68 *dumb-show* pantomime. *suited* dressed.   69–70 *his doublet*

that I have a poor pennyworth in the English. He is a
proper man's picture; but alas! who can converse with
a dumb-show? How oddly he is suited! I think he bought
his doublet in Italy, his round hose in France, his bonnet
in Germany, and his behaviour everywhere.   70

NER.   What think you of the Scottish lord, his neighbour?

POR.   That he hath a neighbourly charity in him; for he borrowed a box of the ear of the Englishman, and swore
he would pay him again when he was able. I think the
Frenchman became his surety and seal'd under for an-   75
other.

NER.   How like you the young German, the Duke of Saxony's
nephew?

POR.   Very vilely in the morning, when he is sober, and most
vilely in the afternoon, when he is drunk. When he is   80
best, he is a little worse than a man; and when he is
worst, he is little better than a beast. An the worst fall
that ever fell, I hope I shall make shift to go without
him.

NER.   If he should offer to choose, and choose the right casket,   85
you should refuse to perform your father's will if you
should refuse to accept him.

POR.   Therefore, for fear of the worst, I pray thee set a deep
glass of Rhenish wine on the contrary casket; for, if the
devil be within and that temptation without, I know   90
he will choose it. I will do anything, Nerissa, ere I will
be married to a sponge.

NER.   You need not fear, lady, the having any of these lords.
They have acquainted me with their determinations;
which is indeed to return to their home, and to trouble   95

. . . *everywhere* The tendency of the English gentleman in Shakespeare's time to
imitate the fashion of every country was often satirized [K].   71 *Scottish lord*
The poverty of the Scots was a perennial source of mockery in England.   75
seal'd . . . another put his seal under the Scot's seal on a bond promising to
pay. Of course the suggestion is that the Frenchman also received a box on the
ear from the Englishman [K].   79-80 *when he is drunk* The drinking habits of
the Danes and the Germans were notorious in Elizabethan times [K].   82 *fall*
happen.   83 *make shift* contrive.

you with no more suit, unless you may be won by some
other sort than your father's imposition, depending on
the caskets.

POR.   If I live to be as old as Sibylla, I will die as chaste as
Diana unless I be obtained by the manner of my father's   100
will. I am glad this parcel of wooers are so reasonable,
for there is not one among them but I dote on his very
absence; and I pray God grant them a fair departure.

NER.   Do you not remember, lady, in your father's time, a
Venetian, a scholar and a soldier, that came hither in   105
company of the Marquis of Montferrat?

POR.   Yes, yes, it was Bassanio. As I think, so was he call'd.

NER.   True, madam. He, of all the men that ever my foolish
eyes look'd upon, was the best deserving a fair lady.

POR.   I remember him well, and I remember him worthy of   110
thy praise.

                Enter a Servingman.

How now? What news?

SERV.   The four strangers seek for you, madam, to take their
leave; and there is a forerunner come from a fifth, the
Prince of Morocco, who brings word the Prince his mas-   115
ter will be here to-night.

POR.   If I could bid the fifth welcome with so good heart as
I can bid the other four farewell, I should be glad of
his approach. If he have the condition of a saint and
the complexion of a devil, I had rather he should shrive   120
me than wive me.
Come, Nerissa. Sirrah, go before.

96–7 *by some other sort* in some other manner.   97 *your father's imposition* that
imposed by your father.   99 *Sibylla* the prophetess, Deiphobe of Cumae, to
whom Apollo promised as many years of life as the grains of sand she held in her hand.
101 *parcel* company, lot (in a contemptuous sense).   104 *in your father's time*
There is a subtle suggestion that Portia's father had not only known Bassanio but
liked him [K].   120 *complexion of a devil* black, the traditional colour of the
devil.

> Whiles we shut the gate upon one wooer, another knocks
> at the door.   *Exeunt.*

◇◇◇◇◇◇◇◇◇◇◇◇◇◇◇◇

[SCENE III. *Venice. A public place.*]

Enter Bassanio *with* Shylock the Jew.

SHY. Three thousand ducats — well.

BASS. Ay, sir, for three months.

SHY. For three months — well.

BASS. For the which, as I told you, Antonio shall be bound.

SHY. Antonio shall become bound — well.   5

BASS. May you stead me? Will you pleasure me? Shall I know
your answer?

SHY. Three thousand ducats for three months, and Antonio
bound.

BASS. Your answer to that.   10

SHY. Antonio is a good man.

BASS. Have you heard any imputation to the contrary?

SHY. Ho, no, no, no, no! My meaning in saying he is a good
man is to have you understand me that he is sufficient.
Yet his means are in supposition. He hath an argosy   15
bound to Tripolis, another to the Indies. I understand,
moreover, upon the Rialto, he hath a third at Mexico,
a fourth for England, and other ventures he hath, squand-
d'red abroad. But ships are but boards, sailors but men;
there be land rats and water rats, land thieves and water 20

I.III. 6 *stead* accommodate.   11 *good* solvent.   14 *sufficient* as a surety.   15
in supposition uncertain.   *argosy* large merchant ship.   17 *Rialto* the famous
bridge in Venice which, with the street in the neighborhood, is the Venetian
Exchange [K].   18–19 *squand'red* unwisely scattered.   20–1 *land . . . thieves* JOHN-
SON; Q¹: "water theeues and land theeues." The "pirates" which follows supports
Johnson's emendation. Such transposition is a common printing error.

thieves — I mean pirates; and then there is the peril of
waters, winds, and rocks. The man is, notwithstanding,
sufficient. Three thousand ducats. I think I may take his
bond.

BASS.   Be assur'd you may.   25

SHY.   I will be assur'd I may; and, that I may be assured, I
will bethink me. May I speak with Antonio?

BASS.   If it please you to dine with us.

SHY.   Yes, to smell pork, to eat of the habitation which your
prophet the Nazarite conjured the devil into! I will buy   30
with you, sell with you, talk with you, walk with you,
and so following; but I will not eat with you, drink with
you, nor pray with you. What news on the Rialto? Who
is he comes here?

Enter Antonio.

BASS.   This is Signior Antonio.   35

SHY.   [*aside*] How like a fawning publican he looks!
I hate him for he is a Christian;
But more for that in low simplicity
He lends out money gratis and brings down
The rate of usance here with us in Venice.   40
If I can catch him once upon the hip,
I will feed fat the ancient grudge I bear him.
He hates our sacred nation, and he rails,
Even there where merchants most do congregate,
On me, my bargains, and my well-won thrift,   45
Which he calls interest. Cursed be my tribe
If I forgive him!

BASS.   Shylock, do you hear?

---

30 *prophet . . . into* The reference is to Christ's sending evil spirits into a herd
of swine; cf. MATTHEW, II, 23.   36 *publican* The "publicani" were Roman tax
collecters, likely to treat Jews with great abuse and thus particularly detested by
them. There may be an allusion also to the publican in LUKE, XVIII, 10–14, who
fawned on God.   37 *for* because.   40 *usance* interest.   41 *upon the hip* at a dis-
advantage; the term is from wrestling, the hold from which the opponent can be
thrown.   45 *thrift* thriving, prosperity — hence, property [K].   48 *store* wealth.

SHY.	I am debating of my present store,
	And by the near guess of my memory
	I cannot instantly raise up the gross 50
	Of full three thousand ducats. What of that?
	Tubal, a wealthy Hebrew of my tribe,
	Will furnish me. But soft! How many months
	Do you desire? — [*To* Antonio] Rest you fair, good
	signior!
	Your worship was the last man in our mouths. 55
ANT.	Shylock, albeit I neither lend nor·borrow
	By taking nor by giving of excess,
	Yet, to supply the ripe wants of my friend,
	I'll break a custom. [*To* Bassanio] Is he yet possess'd
	How much ye would?
SHY.	Ay, ay, three thousand ducats. 60
ANT.	And for three months.
SHY.	I had forgot — three months, you told me so.
	Well then, your bond. And let me see — but hear you:
	Methoughts you said you neither lend nor borrow
	Upon advantage.
ANT.	I do never use it. 65
SHY.	When Jacob graz'd his uncle Laban's sheep —
	This Jacob from our holy Abram was
	(As his wise mother wrought in his behalf)
	The third possessor; ay, he was the third —
ANT.	And what of him? Did he take interest? 70
SHY.	No, not take interest; not, as you would say,
	Directly int'rest. Mark what Jacob did.
	When Laban and himself were compromis'd

50 *gross* full amount.   57 *excess* interest.   58 *ripe* permitting no delay.   59 *possess'd* informed.   65 *Upon advantage* for interest.   66 *When Jacob . . . sheep* Cf. GENESIS, XXX, 31–43.   68 *As his . . . behalf* because of the efforts of his mother in his behalf, her persuading Isaac by fraud to bless his younger son; cf. GENESIS, XXVII.   72 *what Jacob did* Shylock argues that since Jacob received God's blessing for enlarging his property by his skill in breeding sheep, it cannot be sinful to make money breed.   73 *were compromis'd* had come to an agreement.

That all the eanlings which were streak'd and pied
Should fall as Jacob's hire, the ewes, being rank,   75
In end of autumn turned to the rams;
And when the work of generation was
Between these woolly breeders in the act,
The skilful shepherd pill'd me certain wands,
And, in the doing of the deed of kind,   80
He stuck them up before the fulsome ewes,
Who then conceiving, did in eaning time
Fall parti-colour'd lambs, and those were Jacob's.
This was a way to thrive, and he was blest;
And thrift is blessing, if men steal it not.   85

ANT.   This was a venture, sir, that Jacob serv'd for;
A thing not in his power to bring to pass,
But sway'd and fashion'd by the hand of heaven.
Was this inserted to make interest good?
Or is your gold and silver ewes and rams?   90

SHY.   I cannot tell; I make it breed as fast.
But note me, signior.

ANT.   [*aside*]   Mark you this, Bassanio,
The devil can cite Scripture for his purpose.
An evil soul, producing holy witness,
Is like a villain with a smiling cheek,   95
A goodly apple rotten at the heart.
O, what a goodly outside falsehood hath!

SHY.   Three thousand ducats — 'tis a good round sum.
Three months from twelve — then, let me see, the rate —

ANT.   Well, Shylock, shall we be beholding to you?   100

SHY.   Signior Antonio, many a time and oft

---

74 *eanlings* newborn lambs.   *pied* striped.   75 *rank* in heat.   79 *pill'd* stripped
of bark (Q¹: "pyld").   80 *deed of kind* act of nature.   81 *fulsome* fat.   82 *eaning
time* season when lambs are born.   86 *a venture* Antonio does not wish to deny
the morality of Jacob's trick, but he holds that it was of the nature of a commercial venture, such as every merchant undertakes [K].   *serv'd* was a servant.
89 *inserted . . . good* placed in the Bible as a justification for usury.   100 *beholding* beholden, indebted.   102 *rated* berated, rebuked.   103 *usances* interest,
usury.   105 *suff'rance* patient endurance.   *badge . . . tribe* In various nations
of Europe at various times the Jews were required to wear some distinctive

In the Rialto you have rated me
About my moneys and my usances.
Still have I borne it with a patient shrug;
For suff'rance is the badge of all our tribe.   105
You call me misbeliever, cutthroat dog,
And spet upon my Jewish gaberdine,
And all for use of that which is mine own.
Well then, it now appears you need my help.
Go to then, you come to me and you say,   110
"Shylock, we would have moneys." You say so —
You that did void your rheum upon my beard
And foot me as you spurn a stranger cur
Over your threshold. Moneys is your suit.
What should I say to you? Should I not say   115
"Hath a dog money? Is it possible
A cur can lend three thousand ducats?" or
Shall I bend low, and in a bondman's key,
With bated breath and whisp'ring humbleness,
Say this: 120
"Fair sir, you spet on me on Wednesday last;
You spurn'd me such a day; another time
You call'd me dog; and for these courtesies
I'll lend you thus much moneys"?

ANT.   I am as like to call thee so again,   125
To spet on thee again, to spurn thee too.
If thou wilt lend this money, lend it not
As to thy friends — for when did friendship take
A breed for barren metal of his friend?
But lend it rather to thine enemy,   130
Who if he break, thou mayst with better face

---

costume or other mark; this fact gives peculiar significance to Shylock's words
[K].   107 *spet* spat (a common Elizabethan form). *gaberdine* long cloak. In Spain
— but not in England — Jews were required to wear cloaks down to their feet. It
is possible that there was a conventional costume for Jews in the Elizabethan
theatres.   112 *rheum* spittle.   129 *A breed for barren metal* Aristotle remarks
that interest is against nature, since it is unnatural for gold and silver, which are
barren, to have offspring. This argument depends in this case upon a pun, since
the Greek word "tokos" means both "offspring" and "interest for money" [K].
131 *break* go bankrupt.

Exact the penalty.

SHY.   Why, look you, how you storm!
I would be friends with you and have your love,
Forget the shames that you have stain'd me with,
Supply your present wants, and take no doit   135
Of usance for my moneys,
And you'll not hear me. This is kind I offer.

BASS.   This were kindness.

SHY.   This kindness will I show.
Go with me to a notary, seal me there
Your single bond; and, in a merry sport,   140
If you repay me not on such a day,
In such a place, such sum or sums as are
Express'd in the condition, let the forfeit
Be nominated for an equal pound
Of your fair flesh, to be cut off and taken   145
In what part of your body pleaseth me.

ANT.   Content, in faith. I'll seal to such a bond,
And say there is much kindness in the Jew.

BASS.   You shall not seal to such a bond for me!
I'll rather dwell in my necessity.   150

ANT.   Why, fear not, man! I will not forfeit it.
Within these two months — that's a month before
This bond expires — I do expect return
Of thrice three times the value of this bond.

SHY.   O father Abram, what these Christians are,   155
Whose own hard dealing teaches them suspect
The thoughts of others! Pray you tell me this:
If he should break his day, what should I gain
By the exaction of the forfeiture?

135 *doit* a small trifling sum.   140 *single bond* bond without security.   144
nominated for prescribed as.   147 *Content, in faith* Antonio regards the Jew's
proposition as kind, since he has no expectation of incurring the forfeiture. He
believes that it is Shylock's purpose for once to lend money without interest [K].
156 *dealing* F²; Q¹, F¹: "dealings."   163 *extend* show.   165 *And for . . . me not*
in the future be more just to me than you have been heretofore, since I have

A pound of man's flesh taken from a man   160
Is not so estimable, profitable neither,
As flesh of muttons, beefs, or goats. I say,
To buy his favour I extend this friendship.
If he will take it, so; if not, adieu;
And for my love I pray you wrong me not.   165

ANT.   Yes, Shylock, I will seal unto this bond.

SHY.   Then meet me forthwith at the notary's;
Give him direction for this merry bond,
And I will go and purse the ducats straight,
See to my house, left in the fearful guard   170
Of an unthrifty knave, and presently
I'll be with you.

ANT.   Hie thee, gentle Jew.   *Exit* [Shylock].
The Hebrew will turn Christian; he grows kind.

BASS.   I like not fair terms and a villain's mind.

ANT.   Come on. In this there can be no dismay;   175
My ships come home a month before the day.   *Exeunt.*

proved myself ready to stand your friend in the present case [K].   170 *fearful*
dangerous.   171 *knave* servant.   172 *I'll* Q¹; THEOBALD, K: "I will."   174 *fair*
terms . . . mind Both Antonio and Bassanio regard Shylock's proposal as an act
of kindness; Bassanio is suspicious because such kindness comes from a known
villain. Shakespeare has given the audience every reason to believe that there is
little likelihood of Antonio's ever being obliged to pay the forfeit.

Act Two

◇◇

[SCENE I. *Belmont*. Portia's *house*.]

Enter [the Prince *of]* Morocco, *a tawny* Moor, *all in
white, and three or four* Followers *accordingly, with*
Portia, Nerissa, *and their* Train.

MOR.   Mislike me not for my complexion,
The shadowed livery of the burnish'd sun,
To whom I am a neighbour and near bred.
Bring me the fairest creature northward born,
Where Phœbus' fire scarce thaws the icicles,   5
And let us make incision for your love
To prove whose blood is reddest, his or mine.
I tell thee, lady, this aspect of mine
Hath fear'd the valiant. By my love I swear,
The best-regarded virgins of our clime   10
Have lov'd it too. I would not change this hue,
Except to steal your thoughts, my gentle queen.

POR.   In terms of choice I am not solely led
By nice direction of a maiden's eyes.

II.I. 2 *shadowed . . . sun* His dark complexion is the sign that he comes from a
sunny climate, as the livery which the servant wears signifies what lord he follows
[K]. The metaphor is drawn from heraldry. *shadowed* shaded or umbrated, i.e.
black.   5 *Phoebus* the sun God.   6 *make incision* cut the flesh to draw blood.
7 *reddest* a sign of courage.   8 *aspect* face.   9 *fear'd* terrified.   12 *steal your
thoughts* take possession of your favour.   13 *terms* considerations.   14 *nice
direction* foolish or, perhaps, fussy, scrupulous command. Portia means that in

20

Besides, the lott'ry of my destiny   15
Bars me the right of voluntary choosing.
But, if my father had not scanted me,
And hedg'd me by his wit to yield myself
His wife who wins me by that means I told you,
Yourself, renowned Prince, then stood as fair   20
As any comer I have look'd on yet
For my affection.

MOR.   Even for that I thank you.
Therefore I pray you lead me to the caskets
To try my fortune. By this scimitar,
That slew the Sophy and a Persian prince   25
That won three fields of Sultan Solyman,
I would o'erstare the sternest eyes that look,
Outbrave the heart most daring on the earth,
Pluck the young sucking cubs from the she-bear,
Yea, mock the lion when 'a roars for prey,   30
To win thee, lady. But, alas the while!
If Hercules and Lichas play at dice
Which is the better man, the greater throw
May turn by fortune from the weaker hand:
So is Alcides beaten by his page,   35
And so may I, blind Fortune leading me,
Miss that which one unworthier may attain,
And die with grieving.

POR.   You must take your chance;
And either not attempt to choose at all,
Or swear before you choose, if you choose wrong,   40
Never to speak to lady afterward
In way of marriage. Therefore be advis'd.

MOR.   Nor will not. Come, bring me unto my chance.

---

making her choice she is not altogether influenced by the control which a foolish
maiden's eyes are likely to exert over her affection. In the next sentence she
adds that she has not the right to choose, anyway [K].   17 *scanted* restricted.
18 *wit* wise device.   20 *stood* would stand.   25 *Sophy* King of Persia.   26 *fields*
battles. *Sultan Solyman* the Emperor of Turkey.   27 *o'erstare* outstare.   32
Lichas the page of Hercules.   35 *Alcides* Hercules.   *page* POPE; Q¹: "rage."   42
be advis'd consider carefully.   43 *Nor will not* court another lady afterward.

POR.   First, forward to the temple; after dinner
Your hazard shall be made.

MOR.   Good fortune then!   45
To make me blest or cursed'st among men.   *Exeunt*.

◇◇◇◇◇◇◇◇◇◇◇◇◇◇◇◇

[SCENE II. *Venice. A street*.]

Enter [Launcelot] the Clown, *alone*.

LAUN.   Certainly my conscience will serve me to run from this
Jew my master. The fiend is at mine elbow and tempts
me, saying to me, "Gobbo, Launcelot Gobbo, good
Launcelot," or "good Gobbo," or "good Launcelot
Gobbo, use your legs, take the start, run away." My   5
conscience says, "No. Take heed, honest Launcelot; take
heed, honest Gobbo," or, as aforesaid, "honest Launcelot Gobbo, do not run; scorn running with thy heels."
Well, the most courageous fiend bids me pack. "Via!"
says the fiend. "Away!" says the fiend. "For the heavens,   10
rouse up a brave mind," says the fiend, "and run." Well,
my conscience, hanging about the neck of my heart, says
very wisely to me, "My honest friend Launcelot, being
an honest man's son" — or rather an honest woman's
son; for indeed my father did something smack, some-   15
thing grow to, he had a kind of taste — Well, my conscience says, "Launcelot, budge not." "Budge," says the
fiend. "Budge not," says my conscience. "Conscience,"
say I, "you counsel well." "Fiend," say I, "you counsel

II.II. 1 *serve* permit.   9 *pack* be off.   *Via* get going.   10 *For the heavens* for
Heaven's sake.   12 *hanging . . . heart* like a timid wife who will not let her
husband (heart) go.   13 *honest* chaste.   15 *smack* of vice.   16 *grow to* have
a burnt taste, like milk burned at the bottom of a saucepan (an Elizabethan
household expression).   *taste* (a) unpleasant odour (b) taste for other women.   20
To be ruled if I were ruled.   21 *God . . . mark* The original meaning of this
ejaculation is uncertain, but it is often used, as here, to avert the bad omen in-

well." To be rul'd by my conscience, I should stay with 20
the Jew my master, who (God bless the mark!) is a kind
of devil; and, to run away from the Jew, I should be
ruled by the fiend, who (saving your reverence) is the
devil himself. Certainly the Jew is the very devil incarnation; and, in my conscience, my conscience is but a kind 25
of hard conscience to offer to counsel me to stay with the
Jew. The fiend gives the more friendly counsel. I will
run, fiend; my heels are at your commandment; I will
run.

Enter Old Gobbo, *with a basket.*

GOB.   Master young man, you, I pray you, which is the way to 30
       Master Jew's?

LAUN.   [*aside*] O heavens, this is my true-begotten father! who,
       being more than sand-blind, high-gravel-blind, knows
       me not. I will try confusions with him.

GOB.   Master young gentleman, I pray you which is the way to 35
       Master Jew's?

LAUN.   Turn up on your right hand at the next turning, but,
       at the next turning of all, on your left; marry, at the
       very next turning, turn of no hand, but turn down in-
       directly to the Jew's house.   40

GOB.   Be God's sonties, 'twill be a hard way to hit! Can you
       tell me whether one Launcelot that dwells with him,
       dwell with him or no?

LAUN.   Talk you of young Master Launcelot? [*Aside*] Mark me
       now! Now will I raise the waters. — Talk you of young 45
       Master Launcelot?

GOB.   No master, sir, but a poor man's son. His father, though

---

volved in mentioning something disagreeable [K].   **23** *saving your reverence* An
apology for an improper remark.   **24** *incarnation* incarnate.   **33** *sand-blind*
dim-sighted. *high-gravel-blind* stone blind, worse than sand-blind.   **34** *con-
fusions* conclusions.   **41** *Be God's sonties* An old popular oath, the exact meaning of which was no more intelligible to the Elizabethans than it is to us [K].
45 *raise the waters* cause excitement.

I say't, is an honest exceeding poor man, and, God be thanked, well to live.

LAUN. Well, let his father be what 'a will, we talk of young Master Launcelot. 50

GOB. Your worship's friend, and Launcelot, sir.

LAUN. But, I pray you, ergo, old man, ergo, I beseech you, talk you of young Master Launcelot?

GOB. Of Launcelot, an't please your mastership. 55

LAUN. Ergo Master Launcelot. Talk not of Master Launcelot, father; for the young gentleman, according to Fates and Destinies and such odd sayings, the Sisters Three and such branches of learning, is indeed deceased, or, as you would say in plain terms, gone to heaven. 60

GOB. Marry, God forbid! The boy was the very staff of my age, my very prop.

LAUN. [*aside*] Do I look like a cudgel or a hovel-post, a staff, or a prop? — Do you know me, father?

GOB. Alack the day, I know you not, young gentleman! but 65 I pray you tell me, is my boy (God rest his soul!) alive or dead?

LAUN. Do you not know me, father?

GOB. Alack, sir, I am sand-blind! I know you not.

LAUN. Nay, indeed, if you had your eyes, you might fail of the 70 knowing me. It is a wise father that knows his own child. Well, old man, I will tell you news of your son. [*Kneels.*] Give me your blessing. Truth will come to light; murder cannot be hid long — a man's son may, but in the end truth will out. 75

---

49 *well to live* well off in this world's goods. An obvious contradiction of what precedes, and of course intentional on Shakespeare's part, since he represents Old Gobbo as somewhat confused [K].   53 *ergo* therefore — a common term used in formal logical reasoning, as in the schools [K].   55 *an't* if it.   57 *father* old man, a common form of address not necessarily indicating paternity.   58 *Sisters Three* the Fates. Launcelot is trying to take on an elevated style such as a gentleman might use.   63 *hovel-post* post supporting a hovel or shanty.   71–2 *It is . . . child* Launcelot varies the proverb "It is a wise child that knows his own

GOB.   Pray you, sir, stand up. I am sure you are not Launcelot,
my boy.

LAUN.   Pray you let's have no more fooling about it, but give
me your blessing. I am Launcelot — your boy that was,
your son that is, your child that shall be.   80

GOB.   I cannot think you are my son.

LAUN.   I know not what I shall think of that; but I am Launcelot, the Jew's man, and I am sure Margery your wife is
my mother.

GOB.   Her name is Margery indeed. I'll be sworn, if thou be   85
Launcelot, thou art mine own flesh and blood. Lord
worshipp'd might he be! What a beard hast thou got!
Thou hast got more hair on thy chin than Dobbin my
fill-horse has on his tail.

LAUN.   [rises] It should seem then that Dobbin's tail grows   90
backward. I am sure he had more hair of his tail than
I have of my face when I last saw him.

GOB.   Lord, how art thou chang'd! How dost thou and thy
master agree? I have brought him a present. How 'gree
you now?   95

LAUN.   Well, well; but, for mine own part, as I have set up my
rest to run away, so I will not rest till I have run some
ground. My master's a very Jew. Give him a present?
Give him a halter! I am famish'd in his service. You may
tell every finger I have with my ribs. Father, I am glad   100
you are come. Give me your present to one Master
Bassanio, who indeed gives rare new liveries. If I serve
not him, I will run as far as God has any ground. O rare

---

father." 80 *child that shall be* one who will act more like a child in the future.
87 *beard* According to an old stage tradition, Launcelot turns the back of his
head to his father's hand so that his father feels of his long hair and thinks it
is a beard [K]. 89 *fill-horse* cart horse (Q¹: "philhorse"). 96-7 *set up my rest
to* decided to hazard all on (a phrase from the card game called Primero). 98
ground distance. 100 *tell* count. 103 *as far . . . ground* to the end of the
earth.

fortune! here comes the man. To him, father; for I am a
Jew if I serve the Jew any longer.   105

> *Enter* Bassanio, *with* [Leonardo *and*] *a*
> Follower *or two.*

BASS.   You may do so; but let it be so hasted that supper be
ready at the farthest by five of the clock. See these letters
delivered, put the liveries to making, and desire Gratiano
to come anon to my lodging.

> *Exit one of his men.*

LAUN.   To him, father.   110

GOB.   God bless your worship!

BASS.   Gramercy. Wouldst thou aught with me?

GOB.   Here's my son, sir, a poor boy —

LAUN.   Not a poor boy, sir, but the rich Jew's man, that would,
sir, as my father shall specify —   115

GOB.   He hath a great infection, sir, as one would say, to serve —

LAUN.   Indeed, the short and the long is, I serve the Jew, and
have a desire, as my father shall specify —

GOB.   His master and he (saving your worship's reverence) are
scarce cater-cousins.   120

LAUN.   To be brief, the very truth is, that the Jew having done
me wrong, doth cause me, as my father, being, I hope,
an old man, shall frutify unto you —

GOB.   I have here a dish of doves that I would bestow upon
your worship; and my suit is —   125

---

116 *infection* affection, desire. Old Gobbo is trying to use elegant language.   120
scarce (a) scarcely (b) stingy.   *cater-cousins* close friends; i.e. he and his master
do not get along very well.   123 *frutify* certify, or notify.   126 *impertinent*
appurtenant, or pertinent.   131 *defect* effect — purport or upshot.   132 *suit* (a)
request (b) livery, servant's suit of clothes.   134 *preferr'd* recommended.   137
proverb "He that hath the grace of God, hath enough." A part of it applies, says
Launcelot, to Shylock, a part to Bassanio [K].   143 *More guarded* more trimmed
with braid, with a possible allusion to the long trimmed coats worn by fools.
145–6 *Well . . . a fairer* table. Here Hanmer inserts a stage direction, "Looking

LAUN. In very brief, the suit is impertinent to myself, as your
    worship shall know by this honest old man; and, though
    I say it, though old man, yet poor man, my father.

BASS. One speak for both. What would you?

LAUN. Serve you, sir.   130

GOB. That is the very defect of the matter, sir.

BASS. I know thee well; thou hast obtain'd thy suit.
    Shylock thy master spoke with me this day
    And hath preferr'd thee, if it be preferment
    To leave a rich Jew's service to become   135
    The follower of so poor a gentleman.

LAUN. The old proverb is very well parted between my master
    Shylock and you, sir. You have the grace of God, sir,
    and he hath enough.

BASS. Thou speak'st it well. Go, father, with thy son. 140
    Take leave of thy old master and inquire
    My lodging out. [*To a* Servant] Give him a livery
    More guarded than his fellows'. See it done.

LAUN. Father, in. I cannot get a service, no! I have ne'er a
    tongue in my head! Well, [*looks on his palm*] if any 145
    man in Italy have a fairer table which doth offer to
    swear upon a book — ! I shall have good fortune. Go to,
    here's a simple line of life! Here's a small trifle of wives!
    Alas, fifteen wives is nothing! a 'leven widows and nine
    maids is a simple coming-in for one man; and then to 150
    scape drowning thrice, and to be in peril of my life with
    the edge of a feather-bed! Here are simple scapes. Well,

on his own hand." This is certainly correct. Launcelot means that the lines in
his hand mark him out as a favourite of fortune. Palmistry, the science of
divination by the lines of a man's hand, was more or less believed in the Elizabethan age, and has been a favourite kind of amusement ever since [K]. 146
table in palmistry the quadrangle formed by the four main "lines" of the hand.
146–7 *which doth . . . book* In one form of oath it was customary to lay the
hand upon the Bible [K]. 149 *a 'leven* eleven (an Elizabethan spelling). 150
simple coming-in mere trifle in the way of income. Perhaps he expects to get
dowries or fortunes with all these wives [K].

if Fortune be a woman, she's a good wench for this gear.
Father, come. I'll take my leave of the Jew in the
twinkling.   *Exit* [*with* Old Gobbo]. 155

BASS.   I pray thee, good Leonardo, think on this:
These things being bought and orderly bestow'd
Return in haste, for I do feast to-night
My best-esteem'd acquaintance. Hie thee, go.

LEON.   My best endeavours shall be done herein.   160

Enter Gratiano.

GRA.   Where's your master?

LEON.   Yonder, sir, he walks.   *Exit*.

GRA.   Signior Bassanio!

BASS.   Gratiano!

GRA.   I have a suit to you.

BASS.   You have obtain'd it.

GRA.   You must not deny me. I must go with you   165
To Belmont.

BASS.   Why, then you must. But hear thee, Gratiano.
Thou art too wild, too rude, and bold of voice —
Parts that become thee happily enough
And in such eyes as ours appear not faults;   170
But where thou art not known, why, there they show
Something too liberal. Pray thee take pain
To allay with some cold drops of modesty
Thy skipping spirit, lest through thy wild behaviour
I be misconst'red in the place I go to   175
And lose my hopes.

GRA.   Signior Bassanio, hear me.
If I do not put on a sober habit,

---

153 *gear* business: this favour that he has done me in allowing me to leave the
Jew's service for Bassanio's. Possibly, however, "gear" refers to the whole history
that he pretends to have read in the palm of his hand, all of which is fortunate
from his point of view [K].   157 *bestow'd* put away safely.   164 *a suit* Q², F¹; Q¹:
"suit."   169 *Parts* qualities.   171 *show* appear.   172 *liberal* free, unrestrained.

	Talk with respect, and swear but now and then,	
	Wear prayer books in my pocket, look demurely,	
	Nay more, while grace is saying hood mine eyes	180
	Thus with my hat, and sigh, and say amen,	
	Use all the observance of civility	
	Like one well studied in a sad ostent	
	To please his grandam, never trust me more.	

BASS.   Well, we shall see your bearing.   185

GRA.   Nay, but I bar to-night. You shall not gauge me
        By what we do to-night.

BASS.   No, that were pity.
        I would entreat you rather to put on
        Your boldest suit of mirth, for we have friends
        That purpose merriment. But fare you well.   190
        I have some business.

GRA.   And I must to Lorenzo and the rest;
        But we will visit you at supper time.   *Exeunt.*

❖❖❖❖❖❖❖❖❖❖❖❖❖❖

[SCENE III. *Venice.* Shylock's *house.*]

Enter Jessica *and* [Launcelot] the Clown.

JES.   I am sorry thou wilt leave my father so.
        Our house is hell; and thou, a merry devil,
        Didst rob it of some taste of tediousness.
        But fare thee well. There is a ducat for thee;
        And, Launcelot, soon at supper shalt thou see   5
        Lorenzo, who is thy new master's guest.
        Give him this letter; do it secretly;
        And so farewell. I would not have my father
        See me in talk with thee.

173 *modesty* moderation.   183 *one well . . . ostent* one who has taken pains to
adopt a sober and serious appearance [K].   189 *suit of mirth* Shakespeare is
fond of figures from clothing, and particularly of metaphors in accordance with
which his characters clothe themselves in this or that quality or manner [K].
    II.III. 5 *soon at supper* at supper tonight.

LAUN.   Adieu! Tears exhibit my tongue. Most beautiful pagan,   10
         most sweet Jew! if a Christian do not play the knave and
         get thee, I am much deceived. But adieu! These foolish
         drops do something drown my manly spirit. Adieu!

JES.   Farewell, good Launcelot.

                                        Exit [Launcelot].

         Alack, what heinous sin is it in me   15
         To be asham'd to be my father's child!
         But though I am a daughter to his blood,
         I am not to his manners. O Lorenzo,
         If thou keep promise, I shall end this strife,
         Become a Christian and thy loving wife.   *Exit.* 20

❖❖❖❖❖❖❖❖❖❖❖❖❖

         [SCENE IV. *Venice. A street.*]

         Enter Gratiano, Lorenzo, Salerio, *and* Solanio.

LOR.   Nay, we will slink away in supper time,
         Disguise us at my lodging, and return
         All in an hour.

GRA.   We have not made good preparation.

SALER.   We have not spoke us yet of torchbearers.   5

SOLAN.   'Tis vile, unless it may be quaintly ordered,
         And better in my mind not undertook.

LOR.   'Tis now but four o'clock. We have two hours
         To furnish us.

                Enter Launcelot, *with a letter.*

            Friend Launcelot, what's the news?

---

10 *exhibit* inhibit, restrain.   11 *do* Q¹, F¹; F², K: "did." Those who adopt the F²
reading interpret the line as Launcelot's suggestion that Shylock was not her
father; those who follow Q¹ see it as Launcelot foreshadowing her elopement with
Lorenzo.   12–13 *foolish drops* tears.   18 *manners* character.

   II.IV. 1 *in supper time* during supper.   2 *Disguise us* put on masks.   5 *spoke
us* ordered for us.   *torchbearers* common features at Elizabethan masques.   6
quaintly ordered elegantly arranged, carried out with due attention to detail or

LAUN.   An it shall please you to break up this, it shall seem to   10
        signify.

LOR.   I know the hand. In faith, 'tis a fair hand,
        And whiter than the paper it writ on
        Is the fair hand that writ.

GRA.   Love-news, in faith!

LAUN.   By your leave, sir.   15

LOR.   Whither goest thou?

LAUN.   Marry, sir, to bid my old master the Jew to sup to-night
        with my new master the Christian.

LOR.   Hold here, take this [*gives money*]. Tell gentle Jessica
        I will not fail her. Speak it privately.   20
        Go. [*Exit* Launcelot.] Gentlemen,
        Will you prepare you for this masque to-night?
        I am provided of a torchbearer.

SALER. Ay, marry, I'll be gone about it straight.

SOLAN. And so will I.

LOR.   Meet me and Gratiano   25
        At Gratiano's lodging some hour hence.

SALER. 'Tis good we do so.

                        Exeunt [Salerio *and* Solanio].

GRA.   Was not that letter from fair Jessica?

LOR.   I must needs tell thee all. She hath directed
        How I shall take her from her father's house;   30
        What gold and jewels she is furnish'd with;
        What page's suit she hath in readiness.
        If e'er the Jew her father come to heaven,
        It will be for his gentle daughter's sake;

---

finish [K].   8 *o'clock* Q² (a clocke); Q¹: "of clocke."   10 *break up* open.   *this*
a letter.   *seem to signify* probably enlighten you.   12 *hand* handwriting.   17
bid invite.   23 *torchbearer* Each masquerader was regularly accompanied by one
torchbearer [K].   26 *some hour hence* about an hour from now.   34 *gentle*
There is a pun on "gentile," the spelling of the two words not being entirely
distinguished in Shakespeare's time.

And never dare misfortune cross her foot,   35
Unless she do it under this excuse,
That she is issue to a faithless Jew.
Come, go with me; peruse this as thou goest.
Fair Jessica shall be my torchbearer.   *Exeunt.*

◇◆◇◆◇◆◇◆◇◆◇◆◇◆◇

[SCENE V. *Venice. Before* Shylock's *house.*]

Enter [the] Jew [Shylock] *and* [Launcelot,] *his man that
was* the Clown.

SHY.   Well, thou shalt see, thy eyes shall be thy judge,
The difference of old Shylock and Bassanio. —
What, Jessica! — Thou shalt not gormandize
As thou hast done with me — What, Jessica! —
And sleep, and snore, and rend apparel out. —   5
Why, Jessica, I say!

LAUN.   Why, Jessica!

SHY.   Who bids thee call? I do not bid thee call.

LAUN.   Your worship was wont to tell me I could do nothing
without bidding.

            Enter Jessica.

JES.   Call you? What is your will?   10

SHY.   I am bid forth to supper, Jessica.
There are my keys. But wherefore should I go?
I am not bid for love; they flatter me.
But yet I'll go in hate, to feed upon

---

35 *her foot* her path.   37 *issue* child. *faithless* unbelieving, infidel.
II.v. 3 *gormandize* eat lavishly. Launcelot had previously complained of being
starved in Shylock's service.   11 *bid forth* invited out.   14 *feed upon* eat at
the expense of.   18 *dream of money bags* To dream of money was a traditional
sign of ill omen. *to-night* last night.   20 *reproach* approach.   24 *Black Monday*
Easter Monday. Launcelot's prognostication burlesques Shylock's dream of money
bags.   28 *Lock up my doors* Shylock's antipathy towards masquing, music, and

The prodigal Christian. Jessica, my girl,   15
Look to my house. I am right loath to go.
There is some ill a-brewing towards my rest,
For I did dream of money bags to-night.

LAUN.   I beseech you, sir, go. My young master doth expect
your reproach.   20

SHY.   So do I his.

LAUN.   And they have conspired together. I will not say you
shall see a masque; but if you do, then it was not for
nothing that my nose fell a-bleeding on Black Monday
last at six o'clock i' th' morning, falling out that year   25
on Ash Wednesday was four year in th' afternoon.

SHY.   What, are there masques? Hear you me, Jessica.
Lock up my doors; and when you hear the drum
And the vile squealing of the wry-neck'd fife,
Clamber not you up to the casements then,   30
Nor thrust your head into the public street
To gaze on Christian fools with varnish'd faces;
But stop my house's ears — I mean my casements.
Let not the sound of shallow fopp'ry enter
My sober house. By Jacob's staff I swear   35
I have no mind of feasting forth to-night;
But I will go. Go you before me, sirrah.
Say I will come.

LAUN.   I will go before, sir. Mistress, look out at window for all
this.   40
There will come a Christian by
Will be worth a Jewess' eye.   [*Exit.*]

SHY.   What says that fool of Hagar's offspring? ha?

JES.   His words were "Farewell, mistress" — nothing else.

---

dance reflects a Puritan, not a Jewish attitude.   29 *wry-necked fife* Usually thought to be so called on account of the position of the player's head, but uncertain [K].   30 *casements* windows.   32 *varnish'd faces* faces covered with painted masks.   34 *fopp'ry* foolishness.   42 *Jewess' eye* POPE; Q¹: "Iewes eye." 43 *Hager's offspring* an outcast. Hagar was the gentile servant of Sarah, the wife of Abraham; her son was Ishmael who was driven off and became a vagabond.

SHY.   The patch is kind enough, but a huge feeder,   45
Snail-slow in profit, and he sleeps by day
More than the wildcat. Drones hive not with me;
Therefore I part with him, and part with him
To one that I would have him help to waste
His borrowed purse. Well, Jessica, go in.   50
Perhaps I will return immediately.
Do as I bid you; shut doors after you.
Fast bind, fast find —
A proverb never stale in thrifty mind.   *Exit.*

JES.   Farewell; and if my fortune be not crost,   55
I have a father, you a daughter, lost.   *Exit.*

❖❖❖❖❖❖❖❖❖❖❖❖❖❖

[SCENE VI. *Venice. Near* Shylock's *house.*]

Enter the Maskers, Gratiano *and* Salerio.

GRA.   This is the penthouse under which Lorenzo
Desir'd us to make stand.

SALER.   His hour is almost past.

GRA.   And it is marvel he outdwells his hour,
For lovers ever run before the clock.

SALER.   O, ten times faster Venus' pigeons fly   5
To seal love's bonds new-made than they are wont
To keep obliged faith unforfeited!

GRA.   That ever holds. Who riseth from a feast
With that keen appetite that he sits down?
Where is the horse that doth untread again   10

---

45 *patch* fool.   46 *in profit* in doing anything profitable.   47 *wildcat* which
prowls at night and sleeps by day.   53 *Fast* securely.
II.vi. 1 *penthouse* shelter with a sloping roof, i.e. the balcony of the upper
stage in the Elizabethan theatre.   5–7 *O, ten . . . unforfeited* the lover is far
more eager to consummate new love than he is to remain faithful to the old.
Venus' pigeons the doves sacred to the goddess of love, who were supposed to
draw her chariot. "Pigeon" was also a common term for a fool or gull.   *obliged
faith* betrothal bound by contract.   8 *holds* is true.   10 *untread* retrace.   11

His tedious measures with the unbated fire
That he did pace them first? All things that are
Are with more spirit chased than enjoy'd.
How like a younger or a prodigal
The scarfed bark puts from her native bay,   15
Hugg'd and embraced by the strumpet wind!
How like the Prodigal doth she return,
With over-weather'd ribs and ragged sails,
Lean, rent, and beggar'd by the strumpet wind!

Enter Lorenzo.

SALER.   Here comes Lorenzo. More of this hereafter.   20

LOR.   Sweet friends, your patience for my long abode.
Not I, but my affairs, have made you wait.
When you shall please to play the thieves for wives,
I'll watch as long for you then. Approach.
Here dwells my father Jew. Ho! who's within?   25

[*Enter*] Jessica, *above,* [*in boy's clothes*].

JES.   Who are you? Tell me for more certainty,
Albeit I'll swear that I do know your tongue.

LOR.   Lorenzo, and thy love.

JES.   Lorenzo certain, and my love indeed,
For who love I so much? And now who knows   30
But you, Lorenzo, whether I am yours?

LOR.   Heaven and thy thoughts are witness that thou art.

JES.   Here, catch this casket; it is worth the pains.
I am glad 'tis night, you do not look on me,
For I am much asham'd of my exchange.   35
But love is blind, and lovers cannot see

---

tedious measures the elaborate evolutions which horses were trained to perform.
14 *younger* younger son (Q¹, F¹; ROWE, K: "younker"). There is no need for the
emendation, which does not alter the meaning of the line.   15 *scarfed bark* boat
adorned with streamers.   15 *native bay* home port.   17 *Prodigal* from the Bib-
lical parable, LUKE, XV.   18 *over-weather'd* worn or damaged by the weather.   19
beggar'd impoverished.   21 *abode* delay.   24 *watch* wait.   35 *exchange*
into boy's clothes.

          The pretty follies that themselves commit;
          For if they could, Cupid himself would blush
          To see me thus transformed to a boy.

LOR.   Descend, for you must be my torchbearer.   40

JES.   What, must I hold a candle to my shames?
          They in themselves, good sooth, are too too light.
          Why, 'tis an office of discovery, love,
          And I should be obscur'd.

LOR.   So are you, sweet,
          Even in the lovely garnish of a boy.   45
          But come at once;
          For the close night doth play the runaway,
          And we are stay'd for at Bassanio's feast.

JES.   I will make fast the doors, and gild myself
          With some moe ducats, and be with you straight.   50

                         [Exit above.]

GRA.   Now, by my hood, a gentle, and no Jew!

LOR.   Beshrew me but I love her heartily;
          For she is wise, if I can judge of her;
          And fair she is, if that mine eyes be true;
          And true she is, as she hath prov'd herself;   55
          And therefore, like herself, wise, fair, and true,
          Shall she be placed in my constant soul.

              Enter Jessica, [*below*].

          What, art thou come? On, gentlemen! away!
          Our masquing mates by this time for us stay.
                Exit [*with* Jessica *and* Salerio].

                Enter Antonio.

---

37 *pretty* ingenious.   42 *light* frivolous, wanton (a common pun).   43 *'tis an office of discovery* to act as torchbearer is a service which invites discovery, makes me run the risk of being discovered at once [κ].   44 *obscur'd* darkened, hidden. 45 *garnish* ornament, clothes.   47 *close* secret.   *doth . . . runaway* is passing swiftly.   48 *stay'd for* expected.   49 *gild* (a) enrich (b) make guilty.   51 *gentle* gentile (with a pun).   52 *Beshrew me but* let me be cursed unless.   54 *true*

ANT.	Who's there?	60
GRA.	Signior Antonio?	
ANT.	Fie, fie, Gratiano! Where are all the rest?	
	'Tis nine o'clock; our friends all stay for you.	
	No masque to-night. The wind is come about;	
	Bassanio presently will go aboard.	65
	I have sent twenty out to seek for you.	
GRA.	I am glad on't. I desire no more delight	
	Than to be under sail and gone to-night. *Exeunt.*	

◇◇◇◇◇◇◇◇◇◇◇◇◇◇

[SCENE VII. *Belmont.* Portia's *house.*]

Enter Portia, *with* Morocco, *and both their* Trains.

POR.	Go, draw aside the curtains and discover	
	The several caskets to this noble Prince.	
	Now make your choice.	

[*The curtains are drawn aside.*]

MOR.	The first, of gold, who this inscription bears,	
	"Who chooseth me shall gain what many men desire."	5
	The second, silver, which this promise carries,	
	"Who chooseth me shall get as much as he deserves."	
	This third, dull lead, with warning all as blunt,	
	"Who chooseth me must give and hazard all he hath."	
	How shall I know if I do choose the right?	10
POR.	The one of them contains my picture, Prince.	
	If you choose that, then I am yours withal.	
MOR.	Some god direct my judgment! Let me see.	
	I will survey th' inscriptions back again.	

trustworthy.   55 *true* faithful.   58 *gentlemen* Q², F¹; Q¹: "gentleman."   65
presently immediately.
    II.VII. 1 *discover* disclose.   4 *The first* Q², F¹; Q¹: "This first."   *who* Q¹; POPE,
K: "which."   8 *blunt* (a) plain-spoken (b) base.   12 *withal* with it.   14 *back
again* in reverse order.

What says this leaden casket?   15
"Who chooseth me must give and hazard all he hath."
Must give — for what? for lead! hazard for lead?
This casket threatens. Men that hazard all
Do it in hope of fair advantages.
A golden mind stoops not to shows of dross.   20
I'll then nor give nor hazard aught for lead.
What says the silver, with her virgin hue?
"Who chooseth me shall get as much as he deserves."
As must as he deserves? Pause there, Morocco,
And weigh thy value with an even hand.   25
If thou beest rated by thy estimation,
Thou dost deserve enough; and yet enough
May not extend so far as to the lady;
And yet to be afeard of my deserving
Were but a weak disabling of myself.   30
As much as I deserve? Why, that's the lady!
I do in birth deserve her, and in fortunes,
In graces, and in qualities of breeding;
But more than these, in love I do deserve.
What if I stray'd no farther, but chose here?   35
Let's see once more this saying grav'd in gold:
"Who chooseth me shall gain what many men desire."
Why, that's the lady! All the world desires her.
From the four corners of the earth they come
To kiss this shrine, this mortal breathing saint.   40
The Hyrcanian deserts and the vasty wilds
Of wide Arabia are as throughfares now
For princes to come view fair Portia.
The watery kingdom, whose ambitious head

---

20 *shows of dross* outward appearances of worthlessness.   22 *virgin hue* since
silver is the colour of the moon, and Diana, the virgin goddess, is the moon goddess
[K].   25 *weigh* consider.   26 *rated* valued. *estimation* reputation.   30 *disabling*
disparagement.   32 *in birth* by my nobility of birth. *fortunes* wealth.   33
graces pleasing qualities. *qualities* accomplishments.   36 *grav'd* engraved.   41
Hyrcanian deserts a wild region south of the Caspian Sea. *vasty* vast.   42
throughfares thoroughfares.   44 *watery kingdom* the sea. Morocco speaks in extravagant hyperboles appropriate to his oriental manner.   44 *ambitious head*
waves rising higher than normal, as in a storm.   45 *Spets* spits.   46 *spirits*
spirited persons, with a quibble since it was believed that spirits were incapable

Spets in the face of heaven, is no bar   45
To stop the foreign spirits; but they come,
As o'er a brook, to see fair Portia.
One of these three contains her heavenly picture.
Is't like that lead contains her? 'Twere damnation
To think so base a thought. It were too gross   50
To rib her cerecloth in the obscure grave.
Or shall I think in silver she's immur'd,
Being ten times undervalued to tried gold?
O sinful thought! Never so rich a gem
Was set in worse than gold. They have in England   55
A coin that bears the figure of an angel
Stamped in gold — but that's insculp'd upon;
But here an angel in a golden bed
Lies all within. Deliver me the key.
Here do I choose, and thrive I as I may!   60

POR. There, take it, Prince; and if my form lie there,
      Then I am yours.   [*He opens the golden casket.*]

MOR.   O hell! what have we here?
      A carrion Death, within whose empty eye
      There is a written scroll! I'll read the writing.

        All that glisters is not gold —   65
        Often have you heard that told.
        Many a man his life hath sold
        But my outside to behold.
        Gilded tombs do worms infold.
        Had you been as wise as bold,   70
        Young in limbs, in judgment old,

of travelling easily over water.   49 *like* likely.   50 *gross* coarse, valueless.   51
rib her cerecloth cover the waxed cloth in which her body lies, wrapped in lead
[K]. *obscure* dark.   52 *immur'd* walled in.   53 *ten times . . . gold* Gold was
then ten times as valuable as silver. The ratio has much changed since Shakespeare's time [K].   56 *angel* a common Elizabethan gold coin which bore the
figure of the archangel Michael treading on a dragon.   57 *insculp'd* sculptured.
58 *angel . . . bed* Portia's picture in a gold casket.   60 *thrive as I may* let me
have what fortune I can get [K].   61 *form* representation, i.e. picture.   63 *Death*
skull.   68 *outside* either (a) the golden casket or (b) the beautiful face which
once covered the skull.   69 *tombs* JOHNSON; Q¹: "timber."

Your answer had not been inscroll'd.
Fare you well; your suit is cold.

Cold indeed, and labour lost.
Then farewell heat, and welcome frost!   75
Portia, adieu. I have too griev'd a heart
To take a tedious leave. Thus losers part.

Exit [with his Train].

POR.   A gentle riddance. Draw the curtains, go.
Let all of his complexion choose me so.   *Exeunt.*

❖❖❖❖❖❖❖❖❖❖❖❖❖❖

[S C E N E V I I I. *Venice. A street.*]

Enter Salerio *and* Solanio.

SALER.   Why, man, I saw Bassanio under sail;
With him is Gratiano gone along;
And in their ship I am sure Lorenzo is not.

SOLAN.   The villain Jew with outcries rais'd the Duke,
Who went with him to search Bassanio's ship.   5

SALER.   He came too late, the ship was under sail;
But there the Duke was given to understand
That in a gondola were seen together
Lorenzo and his amorous Jessica.
Besides, Antonio certified the Duke   10
They were not with Bassanio in his ship.

SOLAN.   I never heard a passion so confus'd,
So strange, outrageous, and so variable,
As the dog Jew did utter in the streets.
"My daughter! O my ducats! O my daughter!   15

72 *inscroll'd* written on the scroll.   75 *farewell . . . frost* Since the Prince, according to his vow, must never take a wife, he bids farewell to love [K].   77
tedious elaborate, long drawn out.
    II.VIII. 8 *gondola* (Q¹: "Gondylo," K: "gondilo").   9 *amorous* loving or lovable.
12 *passion* fit of emotion.   25 *keep his day* repay the money that he has borrowed of Shylock promptly on the day appointed [K].   27 *reason'd* talked.   28

Fled with a Christian! O my Christian ducats!
Justice! the law! My ducats, and my daughter!
A sealed bag, two sealed bags of ducats,
Of double ducats, stol'n from me by my daughter!
And jewels — two stones, two rich and precious stones,   20
Stol'n by my daughter! Justice! Find the girl!
She hath the stones upon her, and the ducats!"

SALER.   Why, all the boys in Venice follow him,
Crying his stones, his daughter, and his ducats.

SOLAN.   Let good Antonio look he keep his day,   25
Or he shall pay for this.

SALER.   Marry, well rememb'red.
I reason'd with a Frenchman yesterday,
Who told me, in the narrow seas that part
The French and English there miscarried
A vessel of our country richly fraught.   30
I thought upon Antonio when he told me,
And wish'd in silence that it were not his.

SOLAN.   You were best to tell Antonio what you hear.
Yet do not suddenly, for it may grieve him.

SALER.   A kinder gentleman treads not the earth.   35
I saw Bassanio and Antonio part.
Bassanio told him he would make some speed
Of his return; he answered, "Do not so.
Slubber not business for my sake, Bassanio,
But stay the very riping of the time;   40
And for the Jew's bond which he hath of me,
Let it not enter in your mind of love.
Be merry, and employ your chiefest thoughts
To courtship, and such fair ostents of love
As shall conveniently become you there."   45

---

narrow seas the English Channel.   30 *fraught* laden with freight.   39 *Slubber*
perform hastily, bungle (Q², F¹; Q¹: "slumber").   40 *stay . . . time* take as long
as time requires for your business to be completed.   41 *for* as for.   42 *mind of
love* thoughts concerned with love (for Portia).   44 *ostents* expressions, exhibi-
tions.   45 *conveniently* fittingly.

And even there, his eye being big with tears,
Turning his face, he put his hand behind him,
And with affection wondrous sensible
He wrung Bassanio's hand; and so they parted.

SOLAN. I think he only loves the world for him.   50
I pray thee let us go and find him out,
And quicken his embraced heaviness
With some delight or other.

SALER.   Do we so.   *Exeunt.*

❖❖❖❖❖❖❖❖❖❖❖❖❖❖

[SCENE IX. *Belmont.* Portia's *house.*]

Enter Nerissa *and a* Servitor.

NER. Quick, quick, I pray thee; draw the curtain straight.
The Prince of Arragon hath ta'en his oath
And comes to his election presently.

Enter Arragon, *his* Train, *and* Portia
[*with her* Train].

POR. Behold, there stand the caskets, noble Prince.
If you choose that wherein I am contain'd,   5
Straight shall our nuptial rites be solemniz'd;
But if you fail, without more speech, my lord,
You must be gone from hence immediately.

AR. I am enjoin'd by oath to observe three things:
First, never to unfold to any one   10
Which casket 'twas I chose; next, if I fail
Of the right casket, never in my life

---

46 *there* then.   46 *big with* full of.   48 *affection* emotion.   *wondrous sensible*
deeply felt.   50 *loves . . . him* (a) values his possessions so that he may give
them to him (b) lives only for him.   52 *quicken* enliven.   *embraced heaviness*
sadness which he has taken upon himself.
II.ix. 1 *straight* at once.   3 *election* choice.   *presently* immediately.   6 *rites*
POPE; Q¹: "rights."   10 *unfold* disclose.   19 *address'd me* prepared myself.
Fortune good luck.   25 *By* for.   26 *show* outward appearance.   27 *fond* foolish,

To woo a maid in way of marriage;
Lastly,
If I do fail in fortune of my choice,   15
Immediately to leave you and be gone.

POR.   To these injunctions every one doth swear
That comes to hazard for my worthless self.

AR.   And so have I address'd me. Fortune now
To my heart's hope! Gold, silver, and base lead.   20
"Who chooseth me must give and hazard all he hath."
You shall look fairer ere I give or hazard.
What says the golden chest? Ha, let me see!
"Who chooseth me shall gain what many men desire."
What many men desire! That "many" may be meant   25
By the fool multitude, that choose by show,
Not learning more than the fond eye doth teach;
Which pries not to th' interior, but, like the martlet,
Builds in the weather on the outward wall,
Even in the force and road of casualty.   30
I will not choose what many men desire,
Because I will not jump with common spirits
And rank me with the barbarous multitude,
Why then, to thee, thou silver treasure house!
Tell me once more what title thou dost bear.   35
"Who chooseth me shall get as much as he deserves."
And well said too; for who shall go about
To cozen fortune, and be honourable
Without the stamp of merit? Let none presume
To wear an undeserved dignity.   40
O that estates, degrees, and offices
Were not deriv'd corruptly, and that clear honour
Were purchas'd by the merit of the wearer!

---

subject to deception.   28 *martlet* martin, a bird which builds its nest on walls
of buildings.   30 *in the force . . . casualty* subject to the power and in the path
of accident.   32 *jump* be in accord.   37 *go about* undertake.   38 *cozen* cheat.
39 *stamp of merit* official seal to certify genuineness. Arragon is saying that he
will not attempt to cheat Fortune by aspiring to honour without a valid claim
based on his own merit.   41 *estates* property and social status.   *degrees* social
positions.   42 *deriv'd* gained, inherited.   43 *purchas'd* won.

How many then should cover that stand bare!
How many be commanded that command!   45
How much low peasantry would then be gleaned
From the true seed of honour! and how much honour
Pick'd from the chaff and ruin of the times
To be new varnish'd! Well, but to my choice.
"Who chooseth me shall get as much as he deserves."   50
I will assume desert. Give me a key for this,
And instantly unlock my fortunes here.

                    [*He opens the silver casket.*]

POR.   [*aside*] Too long a pause for that which you find there.

AR.   What's here? The portrait of a blinking idiot,
        Presenting me a schedule! I will read it.   55
        How much unlike art thou to Portia!
        How much unlike my hopes and my deservings!
        "Who chooseth me shall have as much as he deserves."
        Did I deserve no more than a fool's head?
        Is that my prize? Are my deserts no better?   60

POR.   To offend and judge are distinct offices
        And of opposed natures.

AR.   What is here?

        The fire seven times tried this.
        Seven times tried that judgment is
        That did never choose amiss.   65
        Some there be that shadows kiss;
        Such have but a shadow's bliss.

---

44 *cover . . . bare* be nobles rather than servants or commoners, since the head
was uncovered by a servant in the presence of his superior.   46 *low peasantry*
persons whose character befits a low rank [K].   46 *gleaned* weeded out. The term
was used not only to apply to the gleaning of corn, but also to the cutting off
of stragglers in battle.   47 *true seed* genuine children.   47–9 *how much . . .
varnish'd* how many men of noble birth, now living in ignoble station, would
be restored to their rightful positions, repainted (new varnish'd) with the outward
show of nobility.   51 *assume desert* take it for granted that I deserve success [K].
61 *To offend . . . offices* the offender should remember that his position is not
that of judge. Portia says this because the Prince, though he has committed a
fault by choosing wrong, is presuming to find fault with the decision of the lot

There be fools alive iwis
Silver'd o'er, and so was this.
Take what wife you will to bed,   70
I will ever be your head.
So be gone; you are sped.

Still more fool I shall appear
By the time I linger here.
With one fool's head I came to woo,   75
But I go away with two.
Sweet, adieu. I'll keep my oath,
Patiently to bear my wroth.

                          [*Exit with his* Train.]

POR.   Thus hath the candle sing'd the moth.
        O, these deliberate fools! When they do choose,   80
        They have the wisdom by their wit to lose.

NER.   The ancient saying is no heresy,
        Hanging and wiving goes by destiny.

POR.   Come draw the curtain, Nerissa.

                Enter Messenger.

MESS.   Where is my lady?

POR.   Here. What would my lord?   85

MESS.   Madam, there is alighted at your gate
        A young Venetian, one that comes before
        To signify th' approaching of his lord;
        From whom he bringeth sensible regreets,
        To wit, besides commends and courteous breath,   90

[K].   63 *this* this silver.   66 *shadows* unsubstantial things (with a possible glance
at the custom of kissing pictures).   67 *shadow's bliss* false happiness, being based
upon nothing substantial.   68 *iwis* certainly.   69 *silver'd o'er* grey-haired and
thus of wise appearance.   71 *I will . . . head* you will always have a fool's head,
always be a fool [K].   72 *you are sped* your fate is settled.   73–4 *Still . . . here*
the longer I linger here, the bigger fool I shall seem [K].   78 *wroth* ruth (a
variant spelling).   81 *They have . . . lose* they are so wise that, when they
have used all their wisdom in deliberating, they choose wrong, and lose [K].   85
my lord said jestingly, of course; Portia is light-headed at her escape from another unwelcome suitor [K].   89 *sensible regreets* greetings that show his deep
feeling [K].   90 *commends* commendations, expressions of respect.

Gifts of rich value. Yet I have not seen
So likely an ambassador of love.
A day in April never came so sweet
To show how costly summer was at hand
As this fore-spurrer comes before his lord.   95

POR.   No more, I pray thee. I am half afeard
Thou wilt say anon he is some kin to thee,
Thou spend'st such high-day wit in praising him.
Come, come, Nerissa; for I long to see
Quick Cupid's post that comes so mannerly.   100

NER.   Bassanio, Lord Love, if thy will it be!   *Exeunt.*

---

92 *likely* promising.   94 *costly* lavish, rich.   95 *fore-spurrer* one who rides ahead.
98 *high-day wit* cleverness that befits the eloquence appropriate to a festival [ĸ].
100 *post* messenger.   101 *Lord Love* Nerissa addresses her prayer to the god of
love, which reminds us afresh of the real state of Portia's affections [ĸ].

Act Three

[SCENE I. *Venice. A street.*]

Enter Solanio *and* Salerio.

SOLAN. Now what news on the Rialto?

SALER. Why, yet it lives there uncheck'd that Antonio hath a
ship of rich lading wrack'd on the narrow seas — the
Goodwins I think they call the place — a very dangerous
flat, and fatal, where the carcases of many a tall ship lie   5
buried, as they say, if my gossip Report be an honest
woman of her word.

SOLAN. I would she were as lying a gossip in that as ever knapp'd
ginger or made her neighbours believe she wept for the
death of a third husband. But it is true, without any   10
slips of prolixity or crossing the plain highway of talk,
that the good Antonio, the honest Antonio — O that I
had a title good enough to keep his name company! —

SALER. Come, the full stop.

III.i. 2 *yet . . . uncheck'd* a report still circulates there without contradiction.
3 *wrack'd* wrecked. *narrow seas* the English Channel.   4 *Goodwins* the Goodwin
Sands, a dangerous shoal in the English Channel off the coast of Kent.   5 *tall*
gallant.   6 *gossip Report* Dame Rumour.   8 *gossip* old lady. *knapp'd* bit off.
Old people carried ginger root and similar things in their pockets or pouches to
nibble at [K].   13 *slips of prolixity* wordy lies. A "slip" was a counterfeit coin
[K]. *crossing . . . talk* violating the plain truth of language. Solanio means that
the report is the mere truth [K].   14 *the full stop* bring your report to an end,
tell us the truth and have done [K].

47

SOLAN. Ha, what sayest thou? Why, the end is, he hath lost a   15
ship.

SALER. I would it might prove the end of his losses.

SOLAN. Let me say amen betimes, lest the devil cross my prayer,
for here he comes in the likeness of a Jew.

Enter Shylock.

How now, Shylock? What news among the merchants?   20

SHY. You knew, none so well, none so well as you, of my
daughter's flight.

SALER. That's certain. I, for my part, knew the tailor that made
the wings she flew withal.

SOLAN. And Shylock, for his own part, knew the bird was fledge;   25
and then it is the complexion of them all to leave the
dam.

SHY. She is damn'd for it.

SALER. That's certain, if the devil may be her judge.

SHY. My own flesh and blood to rebel!   30

SOLAN. Out upon it, old carrion! Rebels it at these years?

SHY. I say my daughter is my flesh and my blood.

SALER. There is more difference between thy flesh and hers
than between jet and ivory; more between your bloods
than there is between red wine and Rhenish. But tell us,   35
do you hear whether Antonio have had any loss at sea
or no?

SHY. There I have another bad match! A bankrout, a prodigal, who dare scarce show his head on the Rialto! a

18 *betimes* quickly. *cross* thwart.   23–4 *knew . . . the wings* knew the person
who contrived her flight. There may be an allusion to the fact that Jessica's disguise (boy's clothes) assisted her to escape [K].   25 *fledge* old enough to fly
(CAPELL; Q¹: "flidge"; Q², F¹: "fledg'd").   26 *complexion* temperament, disposition.
27 *dam* mother bird.   31 *it* flesh and blood (in the sense of sensual appetite, as
Solanio uses it).   35 *Rhenish* Rhine wine (white in colour).   38 *bad match* bad
bargain. To "set a match" meant "to make arrangements for a game," hence to
make any arrangements, any appointments, or any compacts. The first "bad
match" to which Shylock refers is of course his relationship with his daughter
[K].   38 *bankrout* bankrupt.   40 *smug* neatly dressed.   41 *wont* acustomed.

beggar, that was us'd to come so smug upon the mart! 40
Let him look to his bond. He was wont to call me usurer.
Let him look to his bond. He was wont to lend money
for a Christian cursy. Let him look to his bond.

SALER. Why, I am sure, if he forfeit, thou wilt not take his
flesh. What's that good for? 45

SHY. To bait fish withal. If it will feed nothing else, it will
feed my revenge. He hath disgrac'd me, and hind'red me
half a million; laugh'd at my losses, mock'd at my gains,
scorned my nation, thwarted my bargains, cooled my
friends, heated mine enemies — and what's his reason? 50
I am a Jew. Hath not a Jew eyes? Hath not a Jew hands,
organs, dimensions, senses, affections, passions? fed with
the same food, hurt with the same weapons, subject to
the same diseases, healed by the same means, warmed
and cooled by the same winter and summer as a Chris- 55
tian is? If you prick us, do we not bleed? If you tickle
us, do we not laugh? If you poison us, do we not die?
And if you wrong us, shall we not revenge? If we are
like you in the rest, we will resemble you in that. If a
Jew wrong a Christian, what is his humility? Revenge. 60
If a Christian wrong a Jew, what should his sufferance
be by Christian example? Why, revenge. The villainy
you teach me I will execute, and it shall go hard but I
will better the instruction.

Enter a Man *from* Antonio.

MAN. Gentlemen, my master Antonio is at his house, and de- 65
sires to speak with you both.

---

43 *for a Christian cursy* as an act of politeness between Christians [K].   46
withal with.   47 *hind'red* prevented me from earning.   49 *cooled* alienated.   50
heated enraged (so as to make their enmity more violent).   52 *dimensions* bodily
members. *affections* feelings. *passions* strong emotions.   60 *what is his humility*
what kind of Christian humility does he show [K].   63–4 *it shall go . . . instruction* it will be a remarkable thing if I do not succeed in improving on the
lessons that the Christians have taught me about revenge [K]. It should be noted
that this speech, taken by many as a defence of Shylock's behaviour as a natural
reaction to anti-Semitism, is, in fact, Shylock's attempt to justify blood revenge.

SALER.   We have been up and down to seek him.

Enter Tubal.

SOLAN.   Here comes another of the tribe. A third cannot be
match'd, unless the devil himself turn Jew.

Exeunt [Solanio, Salerio, *and* Man].

SHY.   How now, Tubal? What news from Genoa? Hast thou   70
found my daughter?

TUB.   I often came where I did hear of her, but cannot find
her.

SHY.   Why, there, there, there, there! A diamond gone cost
me two thousand ducats in Frankfort! The curse never   75
fell upon our nation till now; I never felt it till now.
Two thousand ducats in that, and other precious, precious jewels. I would my daughter were dead at my foot,
and the jewels in her ear! Would she were hears'd at
my foot, and the ducats in her coffin! No news of them?   80
Why, so — and I know not what's spent in the search.
Why, thou loss upon loss! the thief gone with so much,
and so much to find the thief; and no satisfaction, no
revenge! nor no ill luck stirring but what lights o' my
shoulders; no sighs but o' my breathing; no tears but o'   85
my shedding.

TUB.   Yes, other men have ill luck too. Antonio, as I heard
in Genoa —

SHY.   What, what, what? Ill luck, ill luck?

TUB.   Hath an argosy cast away coming from Tripolis.   90

SHY.   I thank God, I thank God! Is it true? is it true?

TUB.   I spoke with some of the sailors that escaped the wrack.

SHY.   I thank thee, good Tubal. Good news, good news! Ha,
ha! Heard in Genoa?

68–9 *be match'd* be found to match them.   75 *Frankfort* where fine jewelry was
sold at an international fair held twice a year (к: "Frankford").   79 *hears'd* in
a hearse.   84–5 *no ill luck . . . shoulders* Here Shylock shows no awareness of
Antonio's "ill luck," of which he had earlier seemed fully aware.   94 *Heard*
KELLNER; Q¹: "heere"; ROWE, к: "Where." The reading has been much disputed,

TUB.   Your daughter spent in Genoa, as I heard, one night   95
        fourscore ducats.

SHY.   Thou stick'st a dagger in me. I shall never see my gold
        again. Fourscore ducats at a sitting! fourscore ducats!

TUB.   There came divers of Antonio's creditors in my company
        to Venice that swear he cannot choose but break.   100

SHY.   I am very glad of it. I'll plague him; I'll torture him. I
        am glad of it.

TUB.   One of them showed me a ring that he had of your
        daughter for a monkey.

SHY.   Out upon her! Thou torturest me, Tubal. It was my   105
        turquoise; I had it of Leah when I was a bachelor. I
        would not have given it for a wilderness of monkeys.

TUB.   But Antonio is certainly undone.

SHY.   Nay, that's true, that's very true. Go, Tubal, fee me an
        officer; bespeak him a fortnight before. I will have the   110
        heart of him if he forfeit; for, were he out of Venice, I
        can make what merchandise I will. Go, Tubal, and
        meet me at our synagogue; go, good Tubal; at our
        synagogue, Tubal.   *Exeunt.*

<><><><><><><><><><><><>

[SCENE II. *Belmont.* Portia's *house.*]

Enter Bassanio, Portia, Gratiano, *and all their* Trains;
        [Nerissa].

POR.   I pray you tarry; pause a day or two
        Before you hazard; for in choosing wrong

---

but Kellner's conjecture makes perfect sense, since "e" and "d" are easily confused
in Elizabethan handwriting.   100 *break* go bankrupt.   106 *turquoise* ROWE; Q¹:
"Turkies."   *Leah* Shylock's wife.   108 *undone* ruined.   109 *fee me* hire for me.
110 *officer* sheriff's officer, or catchpole, whose duty it was to make arrests for
debt.   *bespeak* order.   112 *make what merchandise* drive what bargain.

I lose your company. Therefore forbear awhile.
There's something tells me (but it is not love)
I would not lose you; and you know yourself   5
Hate counsels not in such a quality.
But lest you should not understand me well —
And yet a maiden hath no tongue but thought —
I would detain you here some month or two
Before you venture for me. I could teach you   10
How to choose right, but then I am forsworn.
So will I never be; so may you miss me;
But if you do, you'll make me wish a sin —
That I had been forsworn. Beshrew your eyes!
They have o'erlook'd me and divided me;   15
One half of me is yours, the other half yours —
Mine own, I would say; but if mine, then yours,
And so all yours! O, these naughty times
Puts bars between the owners and their rights!
And so, though yours, not yours. Prove it so,   20
Let fortune go to hell for it, not I.
I speak too long; but 'tis to peize the time,
To eche it, and to draw it out in length,
To stay you from election.

BASS.   Let me choose;
For as I am, I live upon the rack.   25

POR.   Upon the rack, Bassanio? Then confess
What treason there is mingled with your love.

III.II. 5 *lose* Q²; Q¹: "loose."   6 *quality* manner.   8 *maiden . . . thought* as a
maiden I cannot utter all that is in my mind.   11 *forsworn* perjured.   15 *o'erlook'd* bewitched.   18 *naughty* bad, wicked. The word was not trivial then as
it is now, for it had not been limited to the peccadilloes of children [K].   20
though yours, not yours though belonging to you since I love you, not yours since
you have not yet established legal right to me by passing the casket test. *Prove
it so* if it prove so — that I am not yours.   21 *Let Fortune . . . not I* Fortune is
to be condemned for it, not I [K].   22 *peize* weigh down, thus extend.   23 *eche*
augment.   24 *stay* delay. *election* choosing.   27 *What treason . . . love* Said
mischievously. The torture of the rack was used to make persons confess. Since
he is on the rack Portia suggests that he confess any falsehood that may be
mingled with his affection. We art not to suppose she imagines that he is a mere

BASS.   None but that ugly treason of mistrust,
         Which makes me fear th' enjoying of my love.
         There may as well be amity and life   30
         'Tween snow and fire as treason and my love.

POR.   Ay, but I fear you speak upon the rack,
         Where men enforced do speak anything.

BASS.   Promise me life, and I'll confess the truth.

POR.   Well then, confess and live.

BASS.   "Confess" and "love"   35
         Had been the very sum of my confession.
         O happy torment, when my torturer
         Doth teach me answers for deliverance!
         But let me to my fortune and the caskets.

POR.   Away then! I am lock'd in one of them.   40
         If you do love me, you will find me out.
         Nerissa and the rest, stand all aloof.
         Let music sound while he doth make his choice;
         Then, if he lose, he makes a swanlike end,
         Fading in music. That the comparison   45
         May stand more proper, my eye shall be the stream
         And wat'ry deathbed for him. He may win;
         And what is music then? Then music is
         Even as the flourish when true subjects bow
         To a new-crowned monarch. Such it is   50

man of faults. She speaks jestingly, on the general theory that love is never quite
faithful or disinterested [K].   29 *fear* be apprehensive about.   33 *enforced* under compulsion.   41 *If you do love . . . out* The casket test is not an arbitrary
game of chance; it is emphasized throughout the play that only a true lover can
choose the right casket, and thus Portia is confident that if Bassanio truly loves
her he will succeed.   42 *stand all aloof* It is likely that at this point Nerissa
and the others mount to the gallery where the musicians are seated, both so as
not to obscure the important action below and to join in the coming song as a
chorus.   45 *Fading in Music* as the swan sings just before death.   46–7 *my eye
. . . for him* if he chooses wrong I will drown him with my tears. Portia is quite
aware that the figure is fantastic. She expressly warns us that she is going to
carry out the metaphor to the bitter end [K].   49 *flourish* sound of trumpets.

As are those dulcet sounds in break of day
That creep into the dreaming bridegroom's ear
And summon him to marriage. Now he goes
With no less presence, but with much more love,
Than young Alcides when he did redeem   55
The virgin tribute paid by howling Troy
To the sea monster. I stand for sacrifice;
The rest aloof are the Dardanian wives,
With bleared visages come forth to view
The issue of th' exploit. Go, Hercules!   60
Live thou, I live. With much much more dismay
I view the fight than thou that mak'st the fray.

>   *A Song, the whilst* Bassanio *comments*
>   *on the caskets to himself.*

>   Tell me, where is fancy bred,
>   Or in the heart, or in the head?
>   How begot, how nourished?   65
>   Reply, reply.
>   It is engend'red in the eyes,
>   With gazing fed; and fancy dies
>   In the cradle where it lies.
>   Let us all ring fancy's knell.   70
>   I'll begin it — Ding, dong, bell.

ALL.   Ding, dong, bell.

BASS.   So may the outward shows be least themselves;

51–3 *dulcet sounds . . . marriage* The playing of music under a bridegroom's window on the wedding morning was an ancient custom.   54 *presence* appearance and bearing.   55 *Alcides* Hercules, who rescued Hesione, daughter of King Laomedon of Troy, from a sea monster; he did it not for love of her, however, but for the horses her father had promised him as a reward.   56 *virgin tribute* Hesione. *howling Troy* the lamenting Trojans.   57 *I stand for sacrifice* By this Portia hints to Bassanio that only the chooser of the leaden casket can win her.   58 *Dardanian wives* Trojan women.   61 *Live thou* if you live.   63 *Fancy* foolish love, infatuation.   67 *eyes* F¹; Q¹: "eye."   73 *So may . . . themselves* Bassanio is looking at the caskets. He means that their outward appearance may bear no relation to the excellence of their contents. This thought he dwells on in the speech which follows.   74 *still* always.   76 *season'd* as food

The world is still deceiv'd with ornament.
In law, what plea so tainted and corrupt   75
But, being season'd with a gracious voice,
Obscures the show of evil? In religion,
What damned error but some sober brow
Will bless it, and approve it with a text,
Hiding the grossness with fair ornament?   80
There is no vice so simple but assumes
Some mark of virtue on his outward parts.
How many cowards, whose hearts are all as false
As stairs of sand, wear yet upon their chins
The beards of Hercules and frowning Mars;   85
Who, inward search'd, have livers white as milk!
And these assume but valour's excrement
To render them redoubted. Look on beauty,
And you shall see 'tis purchas'd by the weight,
Which therein works a miracle in nature,   90
Making them lightest that wear most of it.
So are those crisped snaky golden locks
Which make such wanton gambols with the wind
Upon supposed fairness often known
To be the dowry of a second head,   95
The skull that bred them in the sepulchre.
Thus ornament is but the guiled shore
To a most dangerous sea; the beauteous scarf
Veiling an Indian beauty; in a word,
The seeming truth which cunning times put on   100
To entrap the wisest. Therefore, thou gaudy gold,

---

is seasoned with a sauce to hide its true flavour.   77 *Obscures . . . evil* hides
the evil appearance which it ought to have [K].   79 *approve* demonstrate.   81
vice F²; Q¹: "voice."   84 *stairs* F⁴; Q¹: "stayers."   85 *beards . . . Mars* beards (the
symbols of manhood) cut to give the appearance of fierceness.   86 *search'd*
probed.   86 *livers white as milk* the traditional sign of cowardice.   87 *excrement*
outgrowth, i.e. the beard.   88 *redoubted* feared.   91 *lightest* used with the
common quibble on "wanton."   92 *crisped* curled.   93 *make* POPE; Q¹: "maketh";
F¹: "makes."   *wanton* sportive.   95 *dowry . . . head* a wig.   97 *guiled* deceptive.
99 *an Indian beauty* a black beauty, one who would be regarded as beautiful
among the Indians, but whom Europeans would judge to be extremely ugly. It
should be remembered that only fair women were admired by the Elizabethans
[K].   101 *Therefore* Q²; Q¹, F¹: "Therefore then."

Hard food for Midas, I will none of thee;
Nor none of thee, thou pale and common drudge
'Tween man and man: but thou, thou meagre lead,
Which rather threaten'st than dost promise aught,   105
Thy plainness moves me more than eloquence;
And here choose I. Joy be the consequence!

POR.   [aside] How all the other passions fleet to air,
As doubtful thoughts, and rash-embrac'd despair,
And shudd'ring fear, and green-ey'd jealousy!   110
O love, be moderate; allay thy ecstasy;
In measure rain thy joy; scant this excess!
I feel too much thy blessing. Make it less
For fear I surfeit!

BASS.   [opening the leaden casket] What find I here?
Fair Portia's counterfeit! What demigod   115
Hath come so near creation? Move these eyes?
Or whether, riding on the balls of mine,
Seem they in motion? Here are sever'd lips,
Parted with sugar breath. So sweet a bar
Should sunder such sweet friends. Here in her hairs   120
The painter plays the spider; and hath woven
A golden mesh t' entrap the hearts of men
Faster than gnats in cobwebs. But her eyes —
How could he see to do them? Having made one,
Methinks it should have power to steal both his   125
And leave itself unfurnish'd. Yet look, how far
The substance of my praise doth wrong this shadow
In underprizing it, so far this shadow
Doth limp behind the substance. Here's the scroll,

---

102 *Hard . . . Midas* which Midas found, fond though he was of gold, to be too
hard to eat [K].   103 *drudge* silver, the most common currency in Shakespeare's
time.   104 *meagre* poor, without value.   106 *plainness* THEOBALD; Q¹: "paleness."
109 *As* such as.   110 *green-ey'd* a common epithet for jealousy, coming perhaps
from the fact that jealous persons were believed to suffer from jaundice and thus
have greenish-yellow eyes caused by excess of bile.   112 *scant* decrease.   114 *surfeit* sicken from excess.   115 *counterfeit* portrait.   115–16 *What demigod . . .
creation* the painter has come so near to life that he must be at least a demigod [K].
117 *whether* F¹; Q¹: "whither."   119–20 *So sweet . . . friends* no bar, except so
sweet a one as this, should sunder such sweet friends [K].   123 *Faster* more

The continent and summary of my fortune.   130

> You that choose not by the view
> Chance as fair and choose as true.
> Since this fortune falls to you,
> Be content and seek no new.
> If you be well pleas'd with this   135
> And hold your fortune for your bliss,
> Turn you where your lady is
> And claim her with a loving kiss.

A gentle scroll. Fair lady, by your leave;   [*Kisses her.*]
I come by note, to give and to receive.   140
Like one of two contending in a prize,
That thinks he hath done well in people's eyes,
Hearing applause and universal shout,
Giddy in spirit, still gazing in a doubt
Whether those peals of praise be his or no;   145
So, thrice-fair lady, stand I, even so,
As doubtful whether what I see be true,
Until confirm'd, sign'd, ratified by you.

POR.   You see me, Lord Bassanio, where I stand,
Such as I am. Though for myself alone   150
I would not be ambitious in my wish
To wish myself much better, yet for you
I would be trebled twenty times myself,
A thousand times more fair, ten thousand times more
      rich,
That, only to stand high in your account,   155
I might in virtues, beauties, livings, friends,
Exceed account. But the full sum of me

---

securely.   126 *leave itself unfurnish'd* by stealing away both the painter's eyes, the single eye that he had painted would of course remain unfurnished with its fellow, for the painter could not see to complete the picture [K].   127 *substance* subject. *shadow* picture.   129 *substance* reality, i.e. Portia herself.   130 *continent* that which contains.   131 *view* outward appearance.   132 *Chance as fair* may you thrive as well.   136 *hold . . . bliss* regard what has happened to you as your great happiness in life.   140 *by note* according to my instructions (on the scroll).   141 *prize* contest for a prize.   155 *account* estimation.   157 *account* computation.

Is some of something, which, to term in gross,
Is an unlesson'd girl, unschool'd, unpractis'd;
Happy in this, she is not yet so old   160
But she may learn; happier than this,
She is not bred so dull but she can learn;
Happiest of all is that her gentle spirit
Commits itself to yours to be directed,
As from her lord, her governor, her king.   165
Myself and what is mine to you and yours
Is now converted. But now I was the lord
Of this fair mansion, master of my servants,
Queen o'er myself; and even now, but now,
This house, these servants, and this same myself   170
Are yours, my lord's. I give them with this ring;
Which when you part from, lose, or give away,
Let it presage the ruin of your love
And be my vantage to exclaim on you.

BASS.   Madam, you have bereft me of all words,   175
Only my blood speaks to you in my veins;
And there is such confusion in my powers
As, after some oration fairly spoke
By a beloved prince, there doth appear
Among the buzzing pleased multitude,   180
Where every something, being blent together,
Turns to a wild of nothing, save of joy,
Express'd and not express'd. But when this ring
Parts from this finger, then parts life from hence!
O, then be bold to say Bassanio's dead!   185

NER.   My lord and lady, it is now our time
That have stood by and seen our wishes prosper
To cry "good joy." Good joy, my lord and lady!

GRA.   My Lord Bassanio, and my gentle lady,

---

158 *some of something* the portion of a portion (WARBURTON; Q¹: "sume of something"; F¹, K: "sum of nothing"). *term in gross* cite at its full amount.   159
unpractis'd inexperienced.   166 *converted* transferred. *But now* a little while
ago.   174 *vantage* opportunity. *exclaim on* cry out against, accuse.   177 *powers*
of speech.   181 *blent* blended.   182 *wild of nothing* chaos wherein nothing is
discernible [K].   191 *none from me* no more than I wish you.   192-3 *solemnize
. . . faith* hold the wedding.   195 *so* provided that.   199 *for intermission* to

> I wish you all the joy that you can wish;   190
> For I am sure you can wish none from me;
> And when your honours mean to solemnize
> The bargain of your faith, I do beseech you
> Even at that time I may be married too.

BASS.   With all my heart, so thou canst get a wife.   195

GRA.   I thank your lordship, you have got me one.
> My eyes, my lord, can look as swift as yours.
> You saw the mistress, I beheld the maid;
> You lov'd, I lov'd; for intermission
> No more pertains to me, my lord, than you.   200
> Your fortune stood upon the caskets there,
> And so did mine too, as the matter falls;
> For wooing here until I sweat again,
> And swearing till my very roof was dry
> With oaths of love, at last — if promise last —   205
> I got a promise of this fair one here
> To have her love, provided that your fortune
> Achiev'd her mistress.

POR.   Is this true, Nerissa?

NER.   Madam, it is, so you stand pleas'd withal.

BASS.   And do you, Gratiano, mean good faith?   210

GRA.   Yes, faith, my lord.

BASS.   Our feast shall be much honoured in your marriage.

GRA.   We'll play with them the first boy for a thousand ducats.

NER.   What, and stake down?

GRA.   No, we shall ne'er win at that sport, and stake down.   215
> But who comes here? Lorenzo and his infidel?
> What, and my old Venetian friend Salerio?

---

occupy the leisure time that your devotion allowed me [K].   200 *No more . . .
you* My success in love was no more due to my own efforts than your success was
to yours; in both cases we have the caskets to thank [K].   204 *roof* of his mouth
(Q²; Q¹: "rough").   205 *last* hold good.   208 *Achiev'd* won.   209 *so you . . .
withal* provided you are pleased with it [K].   212 *feast* wedding dinner.   214
stake down put up your money (with a bawdy quibble).   216 *infidel* Jessica.

Enter Lorenzo, Jessica, *and* Salerio (*a*
Messenger *from Venice*).

BASS.   Lorenzo and Salerio, welcome hither,
If that the youth of my new int'rest here
Have power to bid you welcome. By your leave,   220
I bid my very friends and countrymen,
Sweet Portia, welcome.

POR.   So do I, my lord.
They are entirely welcome.

LOR.   I thank your honour. For my part, my lord,
My purpose was not to have seen you here;   225
But meeting with Salerio by the way,
He did entreat me, past all saying nay,
To come with him along.

SALER.   I did, my lord,
And I have reason for it. Signior Antonio
Commends him to you.   [*Gives* Bassanio *a letter*.]

BASS.   Ere I ope his letter,   230
I pray you tell me how my good friend doth.

SALER. Not sick, my lord, unless it be in mind;
Nor well, unless in mind. His letter there
Will show you his estate.   *Open the letter.*

GRA.   Nerissa, cheer yond stranger; bid her welcome.   235
Your hand, Salerio. What's the news from Venice?
How doth that royal merchant, good Antonio?
I know he will be glad of our success.
We are the Jasons, we have won the Fleece.

SALER. I would you had won the fleece that he hath lost!   240

POR.   There are some shrewd contents in yond same paper
That steals the colour from Bassanio's cheek:

---

219 *youth . . . here* the fact that I have had an interest (power to command) in
this household for only a short time. Only by his betrothal to Portia has Bassanio
any right to act as host.   221 *very* true.   223 *entirely* sincerely.   227 *past . . .
nay* beyond my power to refuse.   233 *unless in mind* unless his fortitude enables
him to suffer his misfortune.   234 *estate* condition.   239 *Fleece* the Golden

Some dear friend dead; else nothing in the world
Could turn so much the constitution
Of any constant man. What, worse and worse?   245
With leave, Bassanio — I am half yourself,
And I must freely have the half of anything
That this same paper brings you.

BASS.   O sweet Portia,
Here are a few of the unpleasant'st words
That ever blotted paper! Gentle lady,   250
When I did first impart my love to you,
I freely told you all the wealth I had
Ran in my veins — I was a gentleman;
And then I told you true; and yet, dear lady,
Rating myself at nothing, you shall see   255
How much I was a braggart. When I told you
My state was nothing, I should then have told you
That I was worse than nothing; for indeed
I have engag'd myself to a dear friend,
Engag'd my friend to his mere enemy   260
To feed my means. Here is a letter, lady —
The paper as the body of my friend,
And every word in it a gaping wound
Issuing lifeblood. But is it true, Salerio?
Hath all his ventures fail'd? What, not one hit?   265
From Tripolis, from Mexico, and England,
From Lisbon, Barbary, and India?
And not one vessel scape the dreadful touch
Of merchant-marring rocks?

SALER.   Not one, my lord.
Besides, it should appear that, if he had   270
The present money to discharge the Jew,
He would not take it. Never did I know

Fleece, won by Jason.   240 *he* Antonio.   241 *shrewd* cursed, evil.   245 *constant*
self-contained.   246 *With leave* by your leave.   257 *state* estate.   259 *engag'd*
myself placed myself under financial obligation.   260 *mere* utter, unqualified.
262 *as* is as.   265 *Hath* Q¹; ROWE, K: "Have."   269 *merchant-marring* with power
to destroy merchant ships.   271 *present money* ready cash. *discharge* pay off.

A creature that did bear the shape of man
So keen and greedy to confound a man.
He plies the Duke at morning and at night,   275
And doth impeach the freedom of the state
If they deny him justice. Twenty merchants,
The Duke himself, and the magnificoes
Of greatest port have all persuaded with him;
But none can drive him from the envious plea   280
Of forfeiture, of justice, and his bond.

JES.   When I was with him, I have heard him swear
To Tubal and to Chus, his countrymen,
That he would rather have Antonio's flesh
Than twenty times the value of the sum   285
That he did owe him; and I know, my lord,
If law, authority, and power deny not,
It will go hard with poor Antonio.

POR.   Is it your dear friend that is thus in trouble?

BASS.   The dearest friend to me, the kindest man,   290
The best-condition'd and unwearied spirit
In doing courtesies, and one in whom
The ancient Roman honour more appears
Than any that draws breath in Italy.

POR.   What sum owes he the Jew?   295

BASS.   For me three thousand ducats.

POR.   What, no more?
Pay him six thousand, and deface the bond.
Double six thousand and then treble that
Before a friend of this description
Shall lose a hair through Bassanio's fault.   300
First go with me to church and call me wife,
And then away to Venice to your friend!
For never shall you lie by Portia's side
With an unquiet soul. You shall have gold

---

274 *confound* ruin.   276 *impeach* challenge.   278 *magnificoes* great nobles of
Venice.   279 *port* bearing, dignity.   280 *envious* malicious.   291 *best-condition'd* of noblest traits of character.   297 *deface* destroy.   308 *as maids and
widows* as women lamenting their departed lovers.   310 *cheer* disposition.   311

To pay the petty debt twenty times over.   305
When it is paid, bring your true friend along.
My maid Nerissa and myself meantime
Will live as maids and widows. Come, away!
For you shall hence upon your wedding day.
Bid your friends welcome, show a merry cheer;   310
Since you are dear bought, I will love you dear.
But let me hear the letter of your friend.

BASS.   "Sweet Bassanio, my ships have all miscarried, my creditors grow cruel, my estate is very low, my bond to the
Jew is forfeit; and since in paying it, it is impossible I 315
should live, all debts are clear'd between you and I if I
might but see you at my death. Notwithstanding, use
your pleasure. If your love do not persuade you to come,
let not my letter."

POR.   O love, dispatch all business and be gone!   320

BASS.   Since I have your good leave to go away,
    I will make haste; but till I come again,
No bed shall e'er be guilty of my stay,
    Nor rest be interposer 'twixt us twain.   *Exeunt.*

❖❖❖❖❖❖❖❖❖❖❖❖

[SCENE III.
Venice. The street before Shylock's *house.*]

Enter [Shylock] the Jew *and* Solanio *and* Antonio *and
the* Jailer.

SHY.   Jailer, look to him. Tell not me of mercy.
This is the fool that lent out money gratis.
Jailer, look to him.

ANT.   Hear me yet, good Shylock.

---

dear bought by me, at the price of Antonio's misfortune.   313 *miscarried* been
lost.   317–18 *use your pleasure* follow your own inclinations.   323 *No bed . . .
stay* Bassanio takes an oath which is common in old romances — not to sleep until
he has accomplished his undertaking [K].

SHY.   I'll have my bond! Speak not against my bond!
        I have sworn an oath that I will have my bond.   5
        Thou call'dst me dog before thou hadst a cause;
        But, since I am a dog, beware my fangs.
        The Duke shall grant me justice. I do wonder,
        Thou naughty jailer, that thou art so fond
        To come abroad with him at his request.   10

ANT.   I pray thee hear me speak.

SHY.   I'll have my bond. I will not hear thee speak.
        I'll have my bond, and therefore speak no more.
        I'll not be made a soft and dull-ey'd fool,
        To shake the head, relent, and sigh, and yield   15
        To Christian intercessors. Follow not.
        I'll have no speaking; I will have my bond.   *Exit.*

SOLAN. It is the most impenetrable cur
        That ever kept with men.

ANT.   Let him alone.
        I'll follow him no more with bootless prayers.   20
        He seeks my life. His reason well I know:
        I oft deliver'd from his forfeitures
        Many that have at times made moan to me.
        Therefore he hates me.

SOLAN.   I am sure the Duke
        Will never grant this forfeiture to hold.   25

ANT.   The Duke cannot deny the course of law;
        For the commodity that strangers have
        With us in Venice, if it be denied,
        Will much impeach the justice of the state,

III.III.   9 *naughty* wicked.   *fond* foolish.   10 *come abroad . . . request*
Antonio has persuaded the jailer to allow him out of custody, perhaps to visit
Shylock in his company.   14 *dull-ey'd* easily deceived.   19 *kept* resided, associ-
ated.   20 *bootless* unavailing.   23 *made moan* pleaded.   26 *deny* prevent.
27 *commodity* advantageous trade relations [K].   28 *it* the denial of "commodity"
or of the course of law.   29 *much impeach* cast aspersion on by accusation.
30–1 *Since that . . . nations* The point is that since Venice derives its prosperity
from international trade, the Duke cannot interfere with the course of law by
which merchants are protected.   32 *bated* dejected (literally "caused me to lose

Since that the trade and profit of the city   30
Consisteth of all nations. Therefore go.
These griefs and losses have so bated me
That I shall hardly spare a pound of flesh
To-morrow to my bloody creditor.
Well, jailer, on. Pray God Bassanio come   35
To see me pay his debt, and then I care not!   *Exeunt.*

◇◇◇◇◇◇◇◇◇◇◇◇◇◇

[SCENE IV. *Belmont.* Portia's *house.*]

Enter Portia, Nerissa, Lorenzo, Jessica, *and* [Balthasar,]
    a Man of Portia's.

LOR.   Madam, although I speak it in your presence,
You have a noble and a true conceit
Of godlike amity, which appears most strongly
In bearing thus the absence of your lord.
But if you knew to whom you show this honour,   5
How true a gentleman you send relief,
How dear a lover of my lord your husband,
I know you would be prouder of the work
Than customary bounty can enforce you.

POR.   I never did repent for doing good,   10
Nor shall not now; for in companions
That do converse and waste the time together,
Whose souls do bear an egal yoke of love,
There must be needs a like proportion
Of lineaments, of manners, and of spirit;   15

---

weight"). Both senses of the word are implied.

    III.IV. 2 *conceit* conception, understanding.   3 *godlike amity* the highest form of friendship, that between man and man. Probably Portia and Lorenzo have been discussing the traditional Renaissance subject of the relation of love to friendship. 9–10 *you would . . . enforce you* this particular act would make you prouder than any other act which you have undertaken by virtue of your usual goodness could cause you to be [K].   12 *converse* associate. *waste* spend.   13 *egal* equal.   14 *needs* of necessity. *proportion* symmetry, likeness. True friends, according to Renaissance notions, must be equal in all things.   15 *manners* character.

Which makes me think that this Antonio,
Being the bosom lover of my lord,
Must needs be like my lord. If it be so,
How little is the cost I have bestow'd
In purchasing the semblance of my soul   20
From out the state of hellish cruelty!
This comes too near the praising of myself.
Therefore no more of it. Hear other things.
Lorenzo, I commit into your hands
The husbandry and manage of my house   25
Until my lord's return. For mine own part,
I have toward heaven breath'd a secret vow
To live in prayer and contemplation,
Only attended by Nerissa here,
Until her husband and my lord's return.   30
There is a monastery two miles off,
And there we will abide. I do desire you
Not to deny this imposition,
The which my love and some necessity
Now lays upon you.

LOR.   Madam, with all my heart.   35
I shall obey you in all fair commands.

POR.   My people do already know my mind
And will acknowledge you and Jessica
In place of Lord Bassanio and myself.
So fare you well till we shall meet again.   40

LOR.   Fair thoughts and happy hours attend on you!

JES.   I wish your ladyship all heart's content.

POR.   I thank you for your wish, and am well pleas'd

---

17 *lover* friend.   20 *purchasing* redeeming.   *semblance of my soul* Antonio, one
who is the image of Bassanio, whom I love as I love my soul [K].   25 *husbandry*
care and ordering.   33 *deny* refuse.   *imposition* service imposed upon you.   46
honest-true honest and trustworthy.   49 *Padua* THEOBALD; Q¹: "Mantua." The
emendation is accepted by all editors. Padua was a famous centre for the study of
civil law.   *render* deliver.   50 *cousin's hand* F¹; Q¹: "cosin hands."   51 *notes*
memoranda.   52 *imagin'd speed* speed of imagination.   53 *Traject* the
"traghetto," a ferry between Venice and the mainland (ROWE; Q¹, K: "Tranect").

To wish it back on you. Fare you well, Jessica.
            Exeunt [Jessica and Lorenzo].
Now, Balthasar,   45
As I have ever found thee honest-true,
So let me find thee still. Take this same letter,
And use thou all th' endeavour of a man
In speed to Padua. See thou render this
Into my cousin's hand, Doctor Bellario;   50
And look, what notes and garments he doth give thee,
Bring them, I pray thee, with imagin'd speed
Unto the Traject, to the common ferry
Which trades to Venice. Waste no time in words
But get thee gone. I shall be there before thee.   55

BALTH. Madam, I go with all convenient speed.   *Exit.*

POR.   Come on, Nerissa. I have work in hand
That you yet know not of. We'll see our husbands
Before they think of us.

NER.   Shall they see us?

POR.   They shall, Nerissa, but in such a habit   60
That they shall think we are accomplished
With that we lack. I'll hold thee any wager,
When we are both accoutered like young men,
I'll prove the prettier fellow of the two,
And wear my dagger with the braver grace,   65
And speak between the change of man and boy
With a reed voice, and turn two mincing steps
Into a manly stride; and speak of frays
Like a fine bragging youth; and tell quaint lies,
How honourable ladies sought my love,   70
Which I denying, they fell sick and died —
I could not do withal! Then I'll repent,

---

54 *trades to* communicates with.   56 *convenient* appropriate.   59 *Shall they see us* Nerissa suspects that Portia intends to conceal herself or to assume a disguise [K].   60 *habit* costume.   61 *accomplished* furnished.   62 *that we lack* the attributes of masculinity.   63 *accoutered* dressed.   65 *braver* finer.   67 *reed* squeaky, like the note of a reed pipe.   67–8 *turn two . . . stride* my steps then will be twice as big as they are now.   69 *quaint* elaborate.   72 *do withal* do anything about it.

And wish, for all that, that I had not kill'd them.
And twenty of these puny lies I'll tell,
That men shall swear I have discontinued school   75
Above a twelvemonth. I have within my mind
A thousand raw tricks of these bragging Jacks,
Which I will practise.

NER.   Why, shall we turn to men?

POR.   Fie, what a question's that,
If thou wert near a lewd interpreter!   80
But come, I'll tell thee all my whole device
When I am in my coach, which stays for us
At the park gate; and therefore haste away,
For we must measure twenty miles to-day.   *Exeunt.*

❖❖❖❖❖❖❖❖❖❖❖❖❖❖

[SCENE V. *Belmont. A garden.*]

Enter [Launcelot the] Clown *and* Jessica.

LAUN.   Yes, truly; for look you, the sins of the father are to be
laid upon the children. Therefore, I promise you, I fear
you. I was always plain with you, and so now I speak
my agitation of the matter. Therefore be o' good cheer,
for truly I think you are damn'd. There is but one hope   5
in it that can do you any good, and that is but a kind
of bastard hope neither.

JES.   And what hope is that, I pray thee?

LAUN.   Marry, you may partly hope that your father got you
not — that you are not the Jew's daughter.   10

JES.   That were a kind of bastard hope indeed! So the sins

73 *for all that* in spite of that — that I could not prevent their dying.   77 *Jacks*
fellows.   78 *turn to* (a) become (b) give ourselves to.   80 *lewd interpreter* one
ready to take your remark in its ribald sense.   82 *stays* waits.

III.v. 2–3 *fear you* fear for you, since you are the child of an evil father.
4 *agitation* cogitation, opinion.   9 *got* conceived.   19 *enow* enough.   20 *e'en*
Q², F¹; Q¹: "in."   20 *one by another* (a) one off another. He means that Christians

of my mother should be visited upon me.

LAUN. Truly then I fear you are damn'd both by father and
mother. Thus when I shun Scylla, your father, I fall
into Charybdis, your mother. Well, you are gone both   15
ways.

JES. I shall be sav'd by my husband. He hath made me a
Christian.

LAUN. Truly, the more to blame he! We were Christians enow
before, e'en as many as could well live one by another.   20
This making of Christians will raise the price of hogs.
If we grow all to be pork-eaters, we shall not shortly
have a rasher on the coals for money.

Enter Lorenzo.

JES. I'll tell my husband, Launcelot, what you say. Here he
comes.   25

LOR. I shall grow jealous of you shortly, Launcelot, if you
thus get my wife into corners.

JES. Nay, you need not fear us, Lorenzo. Launcelot and I
are out. He tells me flatly there's no mercy for me in
heaven because I am a Jew's daughter; and he says you   30
are no good member of the commonwealth, for in con-
verting Jews to Christians you raise the price of pork.

LOR. I shall answer that better to the commonwealth than
you can the getting up of the Negro's belly. The Moor
is with child by you, Launcelot.   35

LAUN. It is much that the Moor should be more than reason;
but if she be less than an honest woman, she is indeed
more than I took her for.

LOR. How every fool can play upon the word! I think the
best grace of wit will shortly turn into silence, and dis-   40

---

live on each other by making profit out of each other [K]. (b) next to one another.   21 *the price of hogs* since pork is not eaten by orthodox Jews.   23 *rasher*
of bacon.   27 *corners* secret places.   29 *out* not on good terms, having quarrelled.
34 *getting up . . . belly* The allusion has never been properly explained, although
it has been surmized that some topical scandal is being referred to.   37 *honest*
chaste.   40 *best grace of* most becoming form of.

	course grow commendable in none only but parrots. Go in, sirrah; bid them prepare for dinner.
LAUN.	That is done, sir. They have all stomachs.
LOR.	Goodly Lord, what a wit-snapper are you! Then bid them prepare dinner. 45
LAUN.	That is done too, sir. Only 'cover' is the word.
LOR.	Will you cover then, sir?
LAUN.	Not so, sir, neither! I know my duty.
LOR.	Yet more quarrelling with occasion? Wilt thou show the whole wealth of thy wit in an instant? I pray thee under- 50 stand a plain man in his plain meaning. Go to thy fellows, bid them cover the table, serve in the meat, and we will come in to dinner.
LAUN.	For the table, sir, it shall be serv'd in; for the meat, sir, it shall be cover'd; for your coming in to dinner, sir, 55 why, let it be as humours and conceits shall govern.

Exit.

LOR.	O dear discretion, how his words are suited!
	The fool hath planted in his memory
	An army of good words; and I do know
	A many fools, that stand in better place, 60
	Garnish'd like him, that for a tricksy word
	Defy the matter. How cheer'st thou, Jessica?
	And now, good sweet, say thy opinion —
	How dost thou like the Lord Bassanio's wife?
JES.	Past all expressing. It is very meet 65
	The Lord Bassanio live an upright life;
	For, having such a blessing in his lady,

---

43 *stomachs* appetites.   46 *only . . . word* Lorenzo should ask that the table be set (covered) rather than that the meal be prepared, since it already has been. 48 *Not so* I will not cover (put on my hat, an improper act for a servant). Launcelot deliberately takes the meaning of "cover" in the wrong sense.   49 *quarrelling with occasion* abusing the opportunity to pun [K].   56 *as humours . . . govern* as your fancy and ideas shall prompt you [K].   57 *discretion* discrimination.   *suited* dressed up, adapted to the matter in hand.   60 *stand in*

He finds the joys of heaven here on earth;
And if on earth he do not merit it,
In reason he should never come to heaven.   70
Why, if two gods should play some heavenly match,
And on the wager lay two earthly women,
And Portia one, there must be something else
Pawn'd with the other; for the poor rude world
Hath not her fellow.

LOR.   Even such a husband   75
Hast thou of me as she is for a wife.

JES.   Nay, but ask my opinion too of that!

LOR.   I will anon. First let us go to dinner.

JES.   Nay, let me praise you while I have a stomach.

LOR.   No, pray thee, let it serve for table-talk;   80
Then, howsome'er thou speak'st, 'mong other things
I shall disgest it.

JES.   Well, I'll set you forth.   *Exeunt.*

better place have a higher social position.   61 *Garnish'd* with vocabulary.   61–2
for a tricksy . . . matter have no regard for the sense of what they are talking
about, provided they can work in a whimsical pun. This is Shakespeare's little
fling at the punning habit of his time [K].   62 *cheer'st thou* do you feel.   69
merit it POPE; Q¹: "meane it, it."   72 *lay* bet, stake.   74 *Pawn'd* staked.   76
for a F¹; Q¹: "for."   79 *stomach* (a) appetite (b) inclination.   81 *howsom'er*
howsoever (Q¹: "how so mere").   82 *set you forth* praise you greatly.

Act Four

<hr/>

[SCENE 1. *Venice. A court of justice.*]

Enter the Duke, *the* Magnificoes, Antonio, Bassanio, Gratiano, [Solanio, *and others*].

DUKE. What, is Antonio here?

ANT. Ready, so please your Grace.

DUKE. I am sorry for thee. Thou art come to answer
A stony adversary, an inhuman wretch,
Uncapable of pity, void and empty   5
From any dram of mercy.

ANT.   I have heard
Your Grace hath ta'en great pains to qualify
His rigorous course; but since he stands obdurate,
And that no lawful means can carry me
Out of his envy's reach, I do oppose   10
My patience to his fury, and am arm'd
To suffer with a quietness of spirit
The very tyranny and rage of his.

DUKE. Go one, and call the Jew into the court.

<hr/>

IV.i. 6 *dram* tiny bit.   7 *qualify* moderate, soften.   10 *envy* malice.   11 *patience* ability to bear misfortune with confidence in the ultimate goodness and justice of God. This is a Christian notion, not to be confused with classical Stoicism. *arm'd* prepared.   13 *tyranny* violence.   18 *fashion of thy malice* malice of thine, which is but a fashion or way of action which you have assumed, and which does not indicate your evil purpose [K].   20 *remorse* compassion. *strange* unusual (on the assumption that compassion on the part of a Jew would be unusual).   21 *strange apparent cruelty* obvious cruelty in an unusual form.   22 *where*

72

SOLAN.   He is ready at the door; he comes, my lord.   15

Enter Shylock.

DUKE.   Make room, and let him stand before our face.
Shylock, the world thinks, and I think so too,
That thou but leadest this fashion of thy malice
To the last hour of act; and then 'tis thought
Thou'lt show thy mercy and remorse more strange   20
Than is thy strange apparent cruelty;
And where thou now exacts the penalty,
Which is a pound of this poor merchant's flesh,
Thou wilt not only loose the forfeiture,
But, touch'd with humane gentleness and love,   25
Forgive a moiety of the principal,
Glancing an eye of pity on his losses,
That have of late so huddled on his back —
Enow to press a royal merchant down
And pluck commiseration of his state   30
From brassy bosoms and rough hearts of flint,
From stubborn Turks and Tartars, never train'd
To offices of tender courtesy.
We all expect a gentle answer, Jew.

SHY.   I have possess'd your Grace of what I purpose,   35
And by our holy Sabbath have I sworn
To have the due and forfeit of my bond.
If you deny it, let the danger light
Upon your charter and your city's freedom!
You'll ask me why I rather choose to have   40
A weight of carrion flesh than to receive
Three thousand ducats. I'll not answer that!
But say it is my humour, is it answer'd?

---

whereas.   24 *loose* release.   26 *moiety* portion — not necessarily a half, as in modern English.   29 *Enow* enough. *royal merchant* one with a whole kingdom at his disposal.   30 *his state* his condition (Q², F¹; Q¹: "this states").   31 *brassy* impregnable like brass.   31 *flint* Q²; Q¹: "flints."   33 *To offices* in duties.   34 *gentle* with a probable pun on "gentile."   35 *possess'd* informed.   38–9 *let the danger . . . freedom* The point is that Venice can no longer be called a free city if it denies foreigners the rights that its laws secure to them [K].   43 *humour* whim.

What if my house be troubled with a rat,
And I be pleas'd to give ten thousand ducats   45
To have it ban'd? What, are you answer'd yet?
Some men there are love not a gaping pig,
Some that are mad if they behold a cat,
And others, when the bagpipe sings i' th' nose,
Cannot contain their urine; for affection,   50
Mistress of passion, sways it to the mood
Of what it likes or loathes. Now for your answer:
As there is no firm reason to be rend'red
Why he cannot abide a gaping pig,
Why he a harmless necessary cat,   55
Why he a woollen bagpipe — but of force
Must yield to such inevitable shame
As to offend himself, being offended;
So can I give no reason, nor I will not,
More than a lodg'd hate and a certain loathing   60
I bear Antonio, that I follow thus
A losing suit against him. Are you answer'd?

BASS.   This is no answer, thou unfeeling man,
         To excuse the current of thy cruelty!

SHY.   I am not bound to please thee with my answers.   65

BASS.   Do all men kill the things they do not love?

SHY.   Hates any man the thing he would not kill?

BASS.   Every offence is not a hate at first.

SHY.   What, wouldst thou have a serpent sting thee twice?

ANT.   I pray you think you question with the Jew.   70
         You may as well go stand upon the beach
         And bid the main flood bate his usual height;
         You may as well use question with the wolf,

---

46 *ban'd* poisoned.   47 *gaping pig* a roasted suckling pig with an apple or lemon
in its mouth.   50 *affection* one's feelings, likes and dislikes.   51 *Mistress* that
which controls (CAPELL; Q¹: "Maisters").   *passion* strong emotion.   51–2 *sways it
. . . loathes* The meaning is that one's feelings influence one's strongest emotions
to suit the person's whimsical likes and dislikes [K.]   53 *rend'red* returned, given.
56 *woollen* covered with wool, as was common with bagpipes.   56 *of force*
perforce.   60 *lodg'd* deeply rooted.   *certain* fixed.   62 *losing suit* since he will

Why he hath made the ewe bleat for the lamb;
You may as well forbid the mountain pines   75
To wag their high tops and to make no noise
When they are fretten with the gusts of heaven;
You may as well do anything most hard
As seek to soften that — than which what's harder? —
His Jewish heart. Therefore I do beseech you   80
Make no moe offers, use no farther means,
But with all brief and plain conveniency
Let me have judgment, and the Jew his will.

BASS.   For thy three thousand ducats here is six.

SHY.   If every ducat in six thousand ducats   85
Were in six parts, and every part a ducat,
I would not draw them, I would have my bond.

DUKE.   How shalt thou hope for mercy, rend'ring none?

SHY.   What judgment shall I dread, doing no wrong?
You have among you many a purchas'd slave,   90
Which, like your asses and your dogs and mules,
You use in abject and in slavish parts,
Because you bought them. Shall I say to you,
"Let them be free, marry them to your heirs!
Why sweat they under burdens? Let their beds   95
Be made as soft as yours, and let their palates
Be season'd with such viands"? You will answer,
"The slaves are ours." So do I answer you.
The pound of flesh which I demand of him
Is dearly bought, 'tis mine, and I will have it.   100
If you deny me, fie upon your law!
There is no force in the decrees of Venice.
I stand for judgment. Answer. Shall I have it?

DUKE.   Upon my power I may dismiss this court

---

lose his money if his cause is upheld and he takes his pound of flesh.   70 *think
you question* consider that you are disputing.   72 *main flood* great sea.   *bate*
abate, decrease.   74 *bleat* F¹; Q¹: "bleak."   75 *pines* F¹; Q¹: of "pines."   77
fretten fretted, worried, rubbed together.   81 *moe* more.   82 *with all . . . conveniency* with all the brevity and straightforwardness that may be proper [K].   87
draw receive.   92 *parts* duties.   100 *'tis* Q²; F¹, Q¹: "as."   104 *Upon* in accordance
with.

Unless Bellario, a learned doctor,   105
Whom I have sent for to determine this,
Come here to-day.

SOLAN.   My lord, here stays without
A messenger with letters from the doctor,
New come from Padua.

DUKE.   Bring us the letters. Call the messenger.   110

BASS.   Good cheer, Antonio! What, man, courage yet!
The Jew shall have my flesh, blood, bones, and all,
Ere thou shalt lose for me one drop of blood.

ANT.   I am a tainted wether of the flock,
Meetest for death. The weakest kind of fruit   115
Drops earliest to the ground, and so let me.
You cannot better be employ'd, Bassanio,
Than to live still, and write mine epitaph.

Enter Nerissa, [*dressed like a* Lawyer's
Clerk].

DUKE.   Came you from Padua from Bellario?

NER.   From both, my lord. Bellario greets your Grace.   120

[*Presents a letter.*]

BASS.   Why dost thou whet thy knife so earnestly?

SHY.   To cut the forfeiture from that bankrout there.

GRA.   Not on thy sole, but on thy soul, harsh Jew,
Thou mak'st thy knife keen; but no metal can —
No, not the hangman's axe — bear half the keenness   125
Of thy sharp envy. Can no prayers pierce thee?

SHY.   No, none that thou hast wit enough to make.

GRA.   O, be thou damn'd, inexecrable dog,

---

107 *stays* waits. *without* outside.   114 *tainted* diseased. *wether* castrated ram.
122 *bankrout* bankrupt.   123 *Not on thy sole . . . soul* This pun was so common
that it may almost be called an Elizabethan idiom. Hence it was not in the least
calculated to raise a laugh [K].   *sole* HANMER; Q¹: "soule."   125 *hangman's* execu-
tioner's.   *bear* have.   126 *envy* malice.   128 *inexecrable* that cannot be execrated
(cursed) sufficiently (Q¹; F³, K: "inexorable").   129 *for thy life . . . accus'd* if thou

And for thy life let justice be accus'd!
Thou almost mak'st me waver in my faith,   130
To hold opinion with Pythagoras,
That souls of animals infuse themselves
Into the trunks of men. Thy currish spirit
Govern'd a wolf, who, hang'd for human slaughter,
Even from the gallows did his fell soul fleet,   135
And, whilst thou layest in thy unhallowed dam,
Infus'd itself in thee; for thy desires
Are wolvish, bloody, starv'd, and ravenous.

SHY.   Till thou canst rail the seal from off my bond,
Thou but offend'st thy lungs to speak so loud.   140
Repair thy wit, good youth, or it will fall
To cureless ruin. I stand here for law.

DUKE.   This letter from Bellario doth commend
A young and learned doctor to our court.
Where is he?

NER.   He attendeth here hard by   145
To know your answer whether you'll admit him.

DUKE.   With all my heart. Some three or four of you
Go give him courteous conduct to this place.
Meantime the court shall hear Bellario's letter.

[*Clerk reads.*] "Your Grace shall understand that at the   150
receipt of your letter I am very sick; but in the instant
that your messenger came, in loving visitation was with
me a young doctor of Rome — his name is Balthasar. I
acquainted him with the cause in controversy between
the Jew and Antonio the merchant. We turn'd o'er many   155
books together. He is furnished with my opinion, which,
bettered with his own learning (the greatness whereof I
cannot enough commend), comes with him at my impor-

---

art put to death, justice will only be satisfied and can easily endure any accusation
that shall be brought against her on that ground [κ].   131 *hold opinion* agree.
Pythagoras reputed to have taught the doctrine of the transmigration of souls.
135 *fell* cruel.   140 *offend'st* injurest.   152 *in loving visitation* on a friendly
visit.

tunity to fill up your Grace's request in my stead. I
beseech you let his lack of years be no impediment to let   160
him lack a reverend estimation; for I never knew so
young a body with so old a head. I leave him to your
gracious acceptance, whose trial shall better publish his
commendation."

                 Enter Portia *for* Balthasar, [*dressed
                 like a* Doctor of Laws].

DUKE.   You hear the learn'd Bellario what he writes;   165
        And here, I take it, is the doctor come.
        Give me your hand. Come you from old Bellario?

POR.   I did, my lord.

DUKE.   You are welcome; take your place.
        Are you acquainted with the difference
        That holds this present question in the court?   170

POR.   I am informed throughly of the cause.
        Which is the merchant here? and which the Jew?

DUKE.   Antonio and old Shylock, both stand forth.

POR.   Is your name Shylock?

SHY.   Shylock is my name.

POR.   Of a strange nature is the suit you follow;   175
        Yet in such rule that the Venetian law
        Cannot impugn you as you do proceed. —
        You stand within his danger, do you not?

ANT.   Ay, so he says.

POR.   Do you confess the bond?

163–4 *whose trial . . . commendation* if you put him to the test, the experiment
will cause his praises to be proclaimed in better terms than I can command [K].
170 *holds this present question* causes this present suit to be held [K].   171
throughly thoroughly.   176 *in such rule* so according to the rules.   177 *as you
do proceed* in the manner of proceeding you have adopted.   178 *You* Antonio.
within his danger in his power to harm you.   180 *must* will, of course. Shylock,
however, interprets the word in a compulsive sense.   182 *quality* nature.
strain'd constrained, forced.   183 *It droppeth . . . heaven* The Jew has asked
what compulsion is there which makes it possible to say that he "must" be

ANT.   I do.

POR.   Then must the Jew be merciful.   180

SHY.   On what compulsion must I? Tell me that.

POR.   The quality of mercy is not strain'd;
It droppeth as the gentle rain from heaven
Upon the place beneath. It is twice blest —
It blesseth him that gives, and him that takes.   185
'Tis mightiest in the mightiest. It becomes
The throned monarch better than his crown.
His sceptre shows the force of temporal power,
The attribute to awe and majesty,
Wherein doth sit the dread and fear of kings;   190
But mercy is above this sceptred sway;
It is enthroned in the hearts of kings,
It is an attribute to God himself;
And earthly power doth then show likest God's
When mercy seasons justice. Therefore, Jew,   195
Though justice be thy plea, consider this —
That, in the course of justice, none of us
Should see salvation. We do pray for mercy,
And that same prayer doth teach us all to render
The deeds of mercy. I have spoke thus much   200
To mitigate the justice of thy plea;
Which if thou follow, this strict court of Venice
Must needs give sentence 'gainst the merchant there.

SHY.   My deeds upon my head! I crave the law,
The penalty and forfeit of my bond.   205

POR.   Is he not able to discharge the money?

BASS.   Yes, here I tender it for him in the court;

---

merciful. Portia replies that it is the very nature or characteristic quality of mercy that it is not a matter of constraint, but comes spontaneously like the rain from heaven [K].   184 *blest* full of blessing.   194 *show* appear.   197-8 *That in . . . salvation* because of original sin by which all men are guilty at birth; thus their hope of salvation lies in the grace or mercy of God rather than in justice. This is a conventional Christian doctrine which Shakespeare also expresses in MEASURE FOR MEASURE.   204 *My deeds . . . head* Shylock's hope for salvation lies in the justice and probity of his deeds on earth, without regard for original sin.   207 *tender* offer.

	Yea, twice the sum. If that will not suffice,	
	I will be bound to pay it ten times o'er	
	On forfeit of my hands, my head, my heart.	210
	If this will not suffice, it must appear	
	That malice bears down truth. And I beseech you,	
	Wrest once the law to your authority.	
	To do a great right, do a little wrong,	
	And curb this cruel devil of his will.	215

POR. It must not be. There is no power in Venice
Can alter a decree established.
'Twill be recorded for a precedent;
And many an error by the same example
Will rush into the state. It cannot be.   220

SHY. A Daniel come to judgment! yea, a Daniel!
O wise young judge, how I do honour thee!

POR. I pray you let me look upon the bond.

SHY. Here 'tis, most reverend Doctor, here it is.

POR. Shylock, there's thrice thy money off'red thee.   225

SHY. An oath, an oath, I have an oath in heaven!
Shall I lay perjury upon my soul?
No, not for Venice.

POR.   Why, this bond is forfeit;
And lawfully by this the Jew may claim
A pound of flesh, to be by him cut off   230
Nearest the merchant's heart. Be merciful.
Take thrice thy money; bid me tear the bond.

SHY. When it is paid, according to the tenure.
It doth appear you are a worthy judge;
You know the law, your exposition   235
Hath been most sound. I charge you by the law,
Whereof you are a well-deserving pillar,

---

208 *twice* Q¹; RITSON, K: "thrice." 212 *bears down* triumphs over. *truth* honesty. 213 *Wrest once . . . authority* use your authority to release Antonio, even if you have to wrench the law a little to bring it into accord with your decree [K]. 221 *Daniel* The allusion is to the wisdom shown by the youthful Daniel in deciding the case between Susanna and the Elders. The passage is in that part of the book of Daniel which is included in the Apocrypha in King

| | Proceed to judgment. By my soul I swear
There is no power in the tongue of man
To alter me. I stay here on my bond. | 240 |

ANT. Most heartily I do beseech the court
      To give the judgment.

POR.   Why then, thus it is:
      You must prepare your bosom for his knife.

SHY. O noble judge! O excellent young man!

POR. For the intent and purpose of the law   245
      Hath full relation to the penalty,
      Which here appeareth due upon the bond.

SHY. 'Tis very true. O wise and upright judge!
      How much more elder art thou than thy looks!

POR. Therefore lay bare your bosom.

SHY.   Ay, his breast —   250
      So says the bond; doth it not, noble judge?
      Nearest his heart. Those are the very words.

POR. It is so. Are there balance here to weigh
      The flesh?

SHY.   I have them ready.

POR. Have by some surgeon, Shylock, on your charge,   255
      To stop his wounds, lest he do bleed to death.

SHY. Is it so nominated in the bond?

POR. It is not so express'd; but what of that?
      'Twere good you do so much for charity.

SHY. I cannot find it; 'tis not in the bond.   260

POR. You, merchant, have you anything to say?

ANT. But little. I am arm'd and well prepar'd.

James's Version [K].   228 *No, not* Q²; Q¹: "Not, not."   233 *tenure* tenour, substance of the bond's terms.   240 *I stay . . . bond* I abide by the provisions of
my bond [K].   246 *Hath full relation to* fully allows and enforces.   253 *balance*
scales.   255 *on your charge* at your own expense.   257 *nominated* named, prescribed.   262 *arm'd* fortified, prepared.

Give me your hand, Bassanio. Fare you well!
Grieve not that I am fall'n to this for you;
For herein Fortune shows herself more kind   265
Than is her custom. It is still her use
To let the wretched man outlive his wealth
To view with hollow eye and wrinkled brow
An age of poverty; from which ling'ring penance
Of such misery doth she cut me off.   270
Commend me to your honourable wife;
Tell her the process of Antonio's end;
Say how I lov'd you, speak me fair in death;
And when the tale is told, bid her be judge
Whether Bassanio had not once a love.   275
Repent but you that you shall lose your friend,
And he repents not that he pays your debt;
For if the Jew do cut but deep enough,
I'll pay it instantly with all my heart.

BASS.   Antonio, I am married to a wife   280
Which is as dear to me as life itself;
But life itself, my wife, and all the world
Are not with me esteem'd above thy life.
I would lose all, ay, sacrifice them all
Here to this devil, to deliver you.   285

POR.   Your wife would give you little thanks for that
If she were by to hear you make the offer.

GRA.   I have a wife who I protest I love.
I would she were in heaven, so she could
Entreat some power to change this currish Jew.   290

NER.   'Tis well you offer it behind her back.
The wish would make else an unquiet house.

SHY.   [*aside*] These be the Christian husbands! I have a
       daughter —
Would any of the stock of Barrabas

---

266 *still her use* continually her custom.   273 *me fair in death* well of me after
I am dead.   279 *with all my heart* (a) with gratitude (b) with my life. The bitter
pun enhances the pathos of the scene.   281 *Which* who.   294 *Barrabas* the

	Had been her husband rather than a Christian! —	295
	We trifle time. I pray thee pursue sentence.	

POR.   A pound of that same merchant's flesh is thine.
        The court awards it, and the law doth give it.

SHY.   Most rightful judge!

POR.   And you must cut this flesh from off his breast.   300
        The law allows it, and the court awards it.

SHY.   Most learned judge! A sentence! Come, prepare!

POR.   Tarry a little; there is something else.
        This bond doth give thee here no jot of blood;
        The words expressly are "a pound of flesh."   305
        Take then thy bond, take thou thy pound of flesh;
        But in the cutting it if thou dost shed
        One drop of Christian blood, thy lands and goods
        Are, by the laws of Venice, confiscate
        Unto the state of Venice.   310

GRA.   O upright judge! Mark, Jew. O learned judge!

SHY.   Is that the law?

POR.   Thyself shalt see the act;
        For, as thou urgest justice, be assur'd
        Thou shalt have justice more than thou desir'st.

GRA.   O learned judge! Mark, Jew. A learned judge!   315

SHY.   I take this offer then. Pay the bond thrice,
        And let the Christian go.

BASS.   Here is the money.

POR.   Soft!
        The Jew shall have all justice. Soft! no haste.
        He shall have nothing but the penalty.   320

GRA.   O Jew! an upright judge! a learned judge!

POR.   Therefore prepare thee to cut off the flesh.
        Shed thou no blood, nor cut thou less nor more

thief preferred to Jesus in LUKE, XXIII, 18–19. Some also have detected a reference
to Barabas, of Marlowe's JEW OF MALTA.   296 *trifle time* waste time in trifling.
313 *urgest justice* base your plea on justice.   318 *Soft* don't be in a hurry.

But just a pound of flesh. If thou tak'st more
Or less than a just pound — be it but so much   325
As makes it light or heavy in the substance
Or the division of the twentieth part
Of one poor scruple; nay, if the scale do turn
But in the estimation of a hair —
Thou diest, and all thy goods are confiscate.   330

GRA.   A second Daniel! a Daniel, Jew!
Now, infidel, I have you on the hip.

POR.   Why doth the Jew pause? Take thy forfeiture.

SHY.   Give me my principal, and let me go.

BASS. I have it ready for thee; here it is.   335

POR.   He hath refus'd it in the open court.
He shall have merely justice and his bond.

GRA.   A Daniel still say I, a second Daniel!
I thank thee, Jew, for teaching me that word.

SHY.   Shall I not have barely my principal?   340

POR.   Thou shalt have nothing but the forfeiture,
To be so taken at thy peril, Jew.

SHY.   Why, then the devil give him good of it!
I'll stay no longer question.

POR.   Tarry, Jew.
The law hath yet another hold on you.   345
It is enacted in the laws of Venice,
If it be prov'd against an alien
That by direct or indirect attempts
He seeks the life of any citizen,
The party 'gainst the which he doth contrive   350
Shall seize one half his goods; the other half

---

325 *just* exact.   327–8 *twentieth part . . . scruple* one grain; a "scruple" was a
minute portion consisting of twenty grains.   344 *stay . . . question* abide no
further discussion of my suit.   350 *contrive* plot.   352 *privy coffer* personal
treasury of the king; Shakespeare is thinking of the English system in which fines
were paid into the privy treasury.   355 *predicament* situation.   360 *danger*
penalty.   *rehears'd* explained.   370 *humbleness . . . fine* if you bear yourself
humbly, I may be induced to commute the forfeit of half of your goods to a mere

Comes to the privy coffer of the state;
And the offender's life lies in the mercy
Of the Duke only, 'gainst all other voice.
In which predicament I say thou stand'st;   355
For it appears by manifest proceeding
That indirectly, and directly too,
Thou hast contriv'd against the very life
Of the defendant, and thou hast incurr'd
The danger formerly by me rehears'd.   360
Down, therefore, and beg mercy of the Duke.

GRA. Beg that thou mayst have leave to hang thyself!
And yet, thy wealth being forfeit to the state,
Thou hast not left the value of a cord;
Therefore thou must be hang'd at the state's charge.   365

DUKE. That thou shalt see the difference of our spirit,
I pardon thee thy life before thou ask it.
For half thy wealth, it is Antonio's;
The other half comes to the general state,
Which humbleness may drive unto a fine.   370

POR. Ay, for the state, not for Antonio.

SHY. Nay, take my life and all! Pardon not that!
You take my house when you do take the prop
That doth sustain my house. You take my life
When you do take the means whereby I live.   375

POR. What mercy can you render him, Antonio?

GRA. A halter gratis. Nothing else, for God's sake!

ANT. So please my lord the Duke and all the court
To quit the fine for one half of his goods,
I am content; so he will let me have   380
The other half in use, to render it

---

fine [K].   371 *for the state . . . Antonio* Portia carefully points out that the Duke
has no authority to release Shylock from paying half his goods to Antonio [K].
379–80 *To quit . . . content* I am content that he be forgiven (quit) even the fine
which the Duke has suggested as a substitute for the loss of half his goods.
so provided that.   381 *in use* in trust, i.e. to be administered by Antonio until
the death of Shylock, at which time it will pass to Lorenzo, his legitimate heir.

	Upon his death unto the gentleman	
	That lately stole his daughter —	
	Two things provided more: that, for this favour,	
	He presently become a Christian;	385
	The other, that he do record a gift	
	Here in the court of all he dies possess'd	
	Unto his son Lorenzo and his daughter.	
DUKE.	He shall do this, or else I do recant	
	The pardon that I late pronounced here.	390
POR.	Art thou contented, Jew? What dost thou say?	
SHY.	I am content.	
POR.	Clerk, draw a deed of gift.	
SHY.	I pray you give me leave to go from hence.	
	I am not well. Send the deed after me,	
	And I will sign it.	
DUKE.	Get thee gone, but do it.	395
GRA.	In christ'ning shalt thou have two godfathers.	
	Had I been judge, thou shouldst have had ten more,	
	To bring thee to the gallows, not the font.	

Exit [Shylock].

DUKE.	Sir, I entreat you home with me to dinner.	
POR.	I humbly do desire your Grace of pardon.	
	I must away this night toward Padua,	400
	And it is meet I presently set forth.	
DUKE.	I am sorry that your leisure serves you not.	
	Antonio, gratify this gentleman,	
	For in my mind you are much bound to him.	405

Exeunt Duke *and his* Train.

---

385 *presently* immediately.   *become a Christian* Forced conversion to Christianity
was a usual punishment meted out to Jews, usually accompanied by the confisca-
tion of their property. Shakespeare's audience would see the conversion not so
much as a punishment but as an enforced benefit which will make possible the
salvation of Shylock's soul. It is a necessary first step in his redemption.   397
ten more Ten and two would make the ordinary number of a jury. In this passage,
however, the allusion is rather to halberdiers or other officers conducting a

BASS.   Most worthy gentleman, I and my friend
Have by your wisdom been this day acquitted
Of grievous penalties, in lieu whereof,
Three thousand ducats, due unto the Jew,
We freely cope your courteous pains withal.   410

ANT.   And stand indebted, over and above,
In love and service to you evermore.

POR.   He is well paid that is well satisfied;
And I, delivering you, am satisfied,
And therein do account myself well paid.   415
My mind was never yet more mercenary.
I pray you know me when we meet again.
I wish you well, and so I take my leave.

BASS.   Dear sir, of force I must attempt you further.
Take some remembrance of us as a tribute,   420
Not as a fee. Grant me two things, I pray you —
Not to deny me, and to pardon me.

POR.   You press me far, and therefore I will yield.
Give me your gloves, I'll wear them for your sake;

[Bassanio *takes off his gloves*.]

And for your love I'll take this ring from you.   425
Do not draw back your hand. I'll take no more;
And you in love shall not deny me this.

BASS.   This ring, good sir? Alas, it is a trifle!
I will not shame myself to give you this.

POR.   I will have nothing else but only this;   430
And now methinks I have a mind to it.

BASS.   There's more depends on this than on the value.

---

criminal to the scaffold [K].   404 *gratify* reward, pay. *gentleman* Portia.   408
in lieu whereof in return for which.   410 *cope . . . withal* meet your endeavours
with — wish to recompense them with [K].   417 *know me* (a) recognize me, since
I am now disguised (b) consider this an introduction, which will make possible
further acquaintance.   419 *attempt* try to persuade.   424 *Give . . . gloves* probably in order to expose the ring, although the exchange of gloves was a customary
token of friendship.   427 *in love* if you love me [K].

The dearest ring in Venice will I give you,
And find it out by proclamation.
Only for this, I pray you pardon me.   435

POR.   I see, sir, you are liberal in offers.
You taught me first to beg, and now methinks
You teach me how a beggar should be answer'd.

BASS.   Good sir, this ring was given me by my wife;
And when she put it on, she made me vow   440
That I should neither sell nor give nor lose it.

POR.   That 'scuse serves many men to save their gifts.
And if your wife be not a madwoman,
And know how well I have deserv'd this ring,
She would not hold out enemy for ever   445
For giving it to me. Well, peace be with you!

Exeunt [Portia *and* Nerissa].

ANT.   My Lord Bassanio, let him have the ring.
Let his deservings, and my love withal,
Be valued 'gainst your wife's commandëment.

BASS.   Go, Gratiano, run and overtake him.
Give him the ring and bring him, if thou canst,   450
Unto Antonio's house. Away! make haste.

Exit Gratiano.

Come, you and I will thither presently,
And in the morning early will we both
Fly toward Belmont. Come, Antonio.   *Exeunt.* 455

◆◆◆◆◆◆◆◆◆◆◆◆◆◆◆◆◆

[SCENE II. *Venice. A street.*]

Enter Portia *and* Nerissa, [*disguised as before*].

POR.   Inquire the Jew's house out, give him this deed,

---

435 *for this* as for this ring.   448 *withal* at the same time.   451 *bring* escort.
IV.II. 5 *you are well o'erta'en* I am glad to have overtaken you [K].

And let him sign it. We'll away to-night
And be a day before our husbands home.
This deed will be well welcome to Lorenzo.

Enter Gratiano.

GRA. Fair sir, you are well o'erta'en. 5
My Lord Bassanio, upon more advice,
Hath sent you here this ring, and doth entreat
Your company at dinner.

POR.   That cannot be.
His ring I do accept most thankfully,
And so I pray you tell him. Furthermore, 10
I pray you show my youth old Shylock's house.

GRA. That will I do.

NER.   Sir, I would speak with you.
[*Aside to* Portia] I'll see if I can get my husband's ring,
Which I did make him swear to keep for ever.

POR. [*aside to* Nerissa] Thou mayst, I warrant. We shall have
old swearing 15
That they did give the rings away to men;
But we'll outface them, and outswear them too.
[*Aloud*] Away! make haste. Thou know'st where I will
tarry.

NER. Come, good sir, will you show me to this house?

Exeunt.

---

6 *more advice* further consideration.   15 *old* plenty of (a colloquial expression).

Act Five

◇◇◇

[SCENE I. *Belmont. Grounds of* Portia's *house*.]

Enter Lorenzo *and* Jessica.

LOR.   The moon shines bright. In such a night as this,
When the sweet wind did gently kiss the trees
And they did make no noise — in such a night
Troilus methinks mounted the Troyan walls
And sigh'd his soul toward the Grecian tents,   5
Where Cressid lay that night.

JES.   In such a night
Did Thisbe fearfully o'ertrip the dew,
And saw the lion's shadow ere himself,
And ran dismay'd away.

LOR.   In such a night
Stood Dido with a willow in her hand   10
Upon the wild sea-banks, and waft her love
To come again to Carthage.

V.I. 4 *Troilus* the hero of Chaucer's beautiful narrative poem of that name, and the pattern of faithful lovers according to the Elizabethan idea [K]. *Troyan* Trojan. 6 *Cressid* Troilus's unfaithful sweetheart. 7 *Thisbe* the sweetheart of Pyramus, whose love story Shakespeare read in Ovid's METAMORPHOSES. She fled from her place of meeting with Pyramus when frightened by a lion. 8 *shadow ere himself* She saw the reflection of the lion in the waters of a fountain before she saw the lion himself. Chaucer tells the story in THE LEGEND OF GOOD WOMEN, which some have held that Shakespeare had before him when he wrote this passage. 10 *Dido* the forsaken sweetheart of Æneas. *willow* the traditional sign of betrayed or forsaken love. 11 *waft* wafted — i.e. made signs by waving the

JES.   In such a night
Medea gathered the enchanted herbs
That did renew old Æson.

LOR.   In such a night
Did Jessica steal from the wealthy Jew,   15
And with an unthrift love did run from Venice
As far as Belmont.

JES.   In such a night
Did young Lorenzo swear he lov'd her well,
Stealing her soul with many vows of faith,
And ne'er a true one.

LOR.   In such a night   20
Did pretty Jessica (like a little shrew)
Slander her love, and he forgave it her.

JES.   I would out-night you, did no body come;
But, hark, I hear the footing of a man.

                    Enter [Stephano,] *a* Messenger.

LOR.   Who comes so fast in silence of the night?   25

MESS.   A friend.

LOR.   A friend? What friend? Your name, I pray you, friend?

MESS.   Stephano is my name, and I bring word
My mistress will before the break of day
Be here at Belmont. She doth stray about   30
By holy crosses, where she kneels and prays
For happy wedlock hours.

LOR.   Who comes with her?

---

willow branch [K].   13–14 *Medea . . . old Æson* Medea, the sorceress who helped
Jason win the golden fleece, prepared a mixture by which the youth of Æson, the
father of Jason, was restored. This incident, not in Chaucer, is in Ovid's
METAMORPHOSES.   16 *unthrift love* a love without worldly possessions.   23 *out-
night you* better you in this test of comparisons. The dialogue between Jessica
and Lorenzo is a good example of an old form of lyric verse in which two persons
each answer the other until one can answer no more. It may be found in some of
the ECLOGUES of Virgil.   24 *footing* footsteps.   30–1 *She doth . . . crosses* she is
engaged in a pilgrimage from one holy shrine (marked by a cross) to another [K].

MESS.	None but a holy hermit and her maid.
	I pray you, is my master yet return'd?
LOR.	He is not, nor we have not heard from him. 35
	But go we in, I pray thee, Jessica,
	And ceremoniously let us prepare
	Some welcome for the mistress of the house.

Enter [Launcelot, *the*] Clown.

LAUN.	Sola, sola! wo ha, ho! sola, sola!
LOR.	Who calls? 40
LAUN.	Sola! Did you see Master Lorenzo? Master Lorenzo, sola, sola!
LOR.	Leave holloaing, man! Here.
LAUN.	Sola! Where? where?
LOR.	Here! 45
LAUN.	Tell him there's a post come from my master, with his horn full of good news. My master will be here ere morning. [*Exit.*]
LOR.	Sweet soul, let's in, and there expect their coming.
	And yet no matter. Why should we go in? 50
	My friend Stephano, signify, I pray you,
	Within the house, your mistress is at hand
	And bring your music forth into the air.

[*Exit* Stephano.]

How sweet the moonlight sleeps upon this bank!
Here will we sit and let the sounds of music   55
Creep in our ears. Soft stillness and the night

---

39 *Sola* the sound of the postboy's horn which Launcelot imitates.   41–2 *Master . . . Lorenzo* ALDIS WRIGHT; Q¹: "M. Lorenzo & M. Lorenzo"; K: "Master Lorenzo and Mistress Lorenzo."   47 *horn . . . news* Lorenzo compares the horn by which the postboy announced his arrival to the cornucopia or horn of plenty.   48 *morning* ROWE; Q¹: "morning, sweete soule."   49 *Sweet soul, let's* ROWE; Q¹ "lets." *expect* await.   56 *in* into.   57 *Become* befit.   *touches* notes, with a suggestion of the touching of the instrument.   59 *patens* shallow dishes, i.e. tiles.   60 *orb* celestial body.   61 *in his motion . . . sings* makes angelic music by means of the motions through which he goes. The various spheres of Ptolemaic astronomy as they moved about the earth in harmonious though complicated circuits were thought to produce divine music. Such harmony of motion, it was believed, could

Become the touches of sweet harmony.
Sit, Jessica. Look how the floor of heaven
Is thick inlaid with patens of bright gold.
There's not the smallest orb which thou behold'st   60
But in his motion like an angel sings,
Still quiring to the young-ey'd cherubins;
Such harmony is in immortal souls;
But whilst this muddy vesture of decay
Doth grossly close it in, we cannot hear it.   65

[*Enter* Musicians.]

Come, ho, and wake Diana with a hymn!
With sweetest touches pierce your mistress' ear
And draw her home with music.   *Play music.*

JES.   I am never merry when I hear sweet music.

LOR.   The reason is, your spirits are attentive.   70
For do but note a wild and wanton herd,
Or race of youthful and unhandled colts,
Fetching mad bounds, bellowing and neighing loud,
Which is the hot condition of their blood:
If they but hear perchance a trumpet sound,   75
Or any air of music touch their ears,
You shall perceive them make a mutual stand,
Their savage eyes turn'd to a modest gaze
By the sweet power of music. Therefore the poet
Did feign that Orpheus drew trees, stones, and floods,   80
Since naught so stockish, hard, and full of rage
But music for the time doth change his nature.
The man that hath no music in himself,

not exist without a harmony of sound. The theory was, as Lorenzo here explains
the matter, that mortal ears were too dull to hear this music. The poets are full
of references to the music of the spheres [K].   64 *muddy . . . decay* the mortal
body, made of dust and subject to decay.   65 *grossly* with its gross substance, the
body, which interferes with the senses of the immortal soul.   66 *Diana* the moon
goddess.   70 *spirits* senses, faculties of perception.   71 *wanton* uncertain, un-
broken, untrained [K].   72 *unhandled* untamed.   74 *condition* nature.   77
make . . . stand the entire herd stand still at once.   78 *modest* gentle.   80
Orpheus the legendary musician of Thrace, to whose music even trees and stones
listened.   81 *stockish* dull, unfeeling.

Nor is not mov'd with concord of sweet sounds,
Is fit for treasons, stratagems, and spoils;   85
The motions of his spirit are dull as night,
And his affections dark as Erebus.
Let no such man be trusted. Mark the music.

Enter Portia *and* Nerissa.

POR.   That light we see is burning in my hall.
How far that little candle throws his beams!   90
So shines a good deed in a naughty world.

NER.   When the moon shone, we did not see the candle.

POR.   So doth the greater glory dim the less.
A substitute shines brightly as a king
Until a king be by; and then his state   95
Empties itself, as doth an inland brook
Into the main of waters. Music! hark!

NER.   It is your music, madam, of the house.

POR.   Nothing is good, I see, without respéct.
Methinks it sounds much sweeter than by day.   100

NER.   Silence bestows that virtue on it, madam.

POR.   The crow doth sing as sweetly as the lark
When neither is attended; and I think
The nightingale, if she should sing by day
When every goose is cackling, would be thought   105
No better a musician than the wren.
How many things by season season'd are
To their right praise and true perfection!
Peace, ho! The moon sleeps with Endymion,
And would not be awak'd.   *Music ceases.*

---

85 *stratagems* dreadful deeds. *spoils* acts of pillage.   86 *motions* impulses.   87 *Erebus* the dark region between Earth and Hades (F²; Q¹: "Terebus"; F¹: "Erobus").   91 *naughty* wicked.   95 *state* majesty.   97 *main of waters* ocean.   99 *Nothing . . . respect* (a) nothing is absolutely good in itself, but only good with reference to conditions or circumstances (b) nothing is good without our liking (respect) for it — without our thought to make it good.   103 *attended* listened to.   107 *by season season'd are* are ripened or made palatable (season'd) by occurring upon a favourable occasion (season).   109 *Endymion* a mortal shepherd beloved by Diana, the moon goddess. She caused him to sleep forever on Mt. Latmos.   114 *praying*

| LOR. | That is the voice, | 110 |

Or I am much deceiv'd, of Portia.

POR.   He knows me as the blind man knows the cuckoo,
By the bad voice.

LOR.   Dear lady, welcome home.

POR.   We have been praying for our husbands' welfare,
Which speed, we hope, the better for our words.   115
Are they return'd?

LOR.   Madam, they are not yet;
But there is come a messenger before
To signify their coming.

POR.   Go in, Nerissa.
Give order to my servants that they take
No note at all of our being absent hence —   120
Nor you, Lorenzo — Jessica, nor you.

A tucket sounds.

LOR.   Your husband is at hand; I hear his trumpet.
We are no telltales, madam; fear you not.

POR.   This night methinks is but the daylight sick;
It looks a little paler. 'Tis a day   125
Such as the day is when the sun is hid.

Enter Bassanio, Antonio, Gratiano, *and*
their Followers.

BASS.   We should hold day with the Antipodes
If you would walk in absence of the sun.

POR.   Let me give light, but let me not be light;
For a light wife doth make a heavy husband,   130

---

on the pilgrimage which she had pretended to undertake.   115 *Which speed*
who prosper.   121 *tucket* a succession of notes on a trumpet, announcing the
approach of a person of importance [K].   127–8 *We should . . . the sun* We
should be able to have daylight here when our Antipodes do (i.e. when it is night
with us), if you would only go abroad to illumine the earth. Bassanio announces
his arrival with this pretty compliment, not supposing that Portia knows that he
has overheard what she has said in lines 124–6 [K].   129 *not be light* not be unfaithful (a common pun).   130 *heavy* sad. The quibble is continued.

And never be Bassanio so for me.
But God sort all! You are welcome home, my lord.

BASS.   I thank you, madam. Give welcome to my friend.
This is the man, this is Antonio,
To whom I am so infinitely bound.   135

POR.   You should in all sense be much bound to him,
For, as I hear, he was much bound for you.

ANT.   No more than I am well acquitted of.

POR.   Sir, you are very welcome to our house.
It must appear in other ways than words,   140
Therefore I scant this breathing courtesy.

GRA.   [to Nerissa] By yonder moon I swear you do me wrong!
In faith, I gave it to the judge's clerk.
Would he were gelt that had it, for my part,
Since you do take it, love, so much at heart.   145

POR.   A quarrel, ho, already! What's the matter?

GRA.   About a hoop of gold, a paltry ring
That she did give me, whose posy was
For all the world like cutler's poetry
Upon a knife, "Love me, and leave me not."   150

NER.   What talk you of the posy or the value?
You swore to me, when I did give it you,
That you would wear it till your hour of death,
And that it should lie with you in your grave.
Though not for me, yet for your vehement oaths,   155
You should have been respective and have kept it.
Gave it a judge's clerk! No, God's my judge,
The clerk will ne'er wear hair on's face that had it.

GRA.   He will, an if he live to be a man.

---

132 *sort all* dispose of everything.   136 *in all sense* (a) in accordance with all the
dictates of reason [K] (b) in every sense of the word.   138 *acquitted* cleared.
141 *scant* cut short.   141 *breathing* consisting of mere breath, words.   144 *gelt*
gelded.   *for my part* so far as I am concerned.   148 *give me* Q¹; STEEVENS, K:
"give to me."   *posy* a short motto, originally a line of verse (poesy) inscribed
within a ring.   149 *cutler's poetry* short verses often engraved upon the blades

NER.	Ay, if a woman live to be a man.	160

GRA.   Now, by this hand, I gave it to a youth,
A kind of boy, a little scrubbed boy,
No higher than thyself, the judge's clerk,
A prating boy that begg'd it as a fee.
I could not for my heart deny it him.   165

POR.   You were to blame — I must be plain with you —
To part so slightly with your wife's first gift,
A thing stuck on with oaths upon your finger
And so riveted with faith unto your flesh.
I gave my love a ring, and made him swear   170
Never to part with it; and here he stands.
I dare be sworn for him he would not leave it
Nor pluck it from his finger for the wealth
That the world masters. Now, in faith, Gratiano,
You give your wife too unkind a cause of grief.   175
An 'twere to me, I should be mad at it.

BASS.   [aside] Why, I were best to cut my left hand off
And swear I lost the ring defending it.

GRA.   My Lord Bassanio gave his ring away
Unto the judge that begg'd it, and indeed   180
Deserv'd it too; and then the boy, his clerk,
That took some pains in writing, he begg'd mine;
And neither man nor master would take aught
But the two rings.

POR.   What ring gave you, my lord?
Not that, I hope, which you receiv'd of me.   185

BASS.   If I could add a lie unto a fault,
I would deny it; but you see my finger
Hath not the ring upon it — it is gone.

POR.   Even so void is your false heart of truth.

---

of fruit knives.   151 *What* why.   152 *give it* Q², F¹; Q¹: "give."   156 *respective* regardful (of your oath).   162 *scrubbed* scrubby, stunted.   164 *prating* talkative. 166 *to blame* culpable.   176 *mad* frantic — not merely angry.   182 *That took . . . writing* that had done some service as a scribe or clerk, and so deserved a reward [K].

By heaven, I will ne'er come in your bed   190
Until I see the ring!

NER.   Nor I in yours
Till I again see mine!

BASS.   Sweet Portia,
If you did know to whom I gave the ring,
If you did know for whom I gave the ring,
And would conceive for what I gave the ring,   195
And how unwillingly I left the ring
When naught would be accepted but the ring,
You would abate the strength of your displeasure.

POR.   If you had known the virtue of the ring,
Or half her worthiness that gave the ring,   200
Or your own honour to contain the ring,
You would not then have parted with the ring.
What man is there so much unreasonable,
If you had pleas'd to have defended it
With any terms of zeal, wanted the modesty   205
To urge the thing held as a ceremony?
Nerissa teaches me what to believe.
I'll die for't but some woman had the ring!

BASS.   No, by my honour, madam, by my soul,
No woman had it, but a civil doctor,   210
Which did refuse three thousand ducats of me
And begg'd the ring; the which I did deny him,
And suffer'd him to go displeas'd away,
Even he that had held up the very life
Of my dear friend. What should I say, sweet lady? 215
I was enforc'd to send it after him.
I was beset with shame and courtesy.
My honour would not let ingratitude

---

195 *And would conceive* and would only give yourself the trouble of really understanding [K].   199 *virtue* power.   201 *contain* withhold.   205–6 *wanted . . .
urge* was so immodest or inconsiderate as to press for the possession of, to insist
on [K].   206 *ceremony* sacred object, symbol.   210 *civil doctor* doctor of civil law,
lawyer.   211 *Which* who.   213 *suffer'd* permitted.   216 *enforc'd* obliged.   217
I was beset . . . courtesy feelings of shame and of regard for politeness both

So much besmear it. Pardon me, good lady;
For, by these blessed candles of the night,   220
Had you been there, I think you would have begg'd
The ring of me to give the worthy doctor.

POR.   Let not that doctor e'er come near my house.
Since he hath got the jewel that I lov'd,
And that which you did swear to keep for me,   225
I will become as liberal as you;
I'll not deny him anything I have,
No, not my body, nor my husband's bed.
Know him I shall, I am well sure of it.
Lie not a night from home; watch me like Argus.   230
If you do not, if I be left alone,
Now, by mine honour, which is yet mine own,
I'll have that doctor for my bedfellow.

NER.   And I his clerk. Therefore be well advis'd
How you do leave me to mine own protection.   235

GRA.   Well, do you so. Let not me take him then;
For if I do, I'll mar the young clerk's pen.

ANT.   I am th' unhappy subject of these quarrels.

POR.   Sir, grieve not you. You are welcome notwithstanding.

BASS.   Portia, forgive me this enforced wrong,   240
And in the hearing of these many friends
I swear to thee, even by thine own fair eyes,
Wherein I see myself —

POR.   Mark you but that?
In both my eyes he doubly sees himself;
In each eye one. Swear by your double self,   245
And there's an oath of credit.

BASS.   Nay, but hear me.

---

attacked me [K].   220 *blessed . . . night* stars (a conventional metaphor).   226
liberal (a) generous (b) sexually promiscuous.   230 *Argus* a mythological creature
with a hundred eyes.   234 *well advis'd* very careful.   237 *pen* instrument, with
a ribald double sense.   240 *enforced wrong* wrongful act committed under
compulsion.   245 *double self* (a) twofold, being reflected in both eyes (b) de-
ceitful.   246 *oath of credit* an oath that may well be believed. Said ironically [K].

           Pardon this fault, and by my soul I swear
           I never more will break an oath with thee.

ANT.   I once did lend my body for his wealth,
           Which, but for him that had your husband's ring,   250
           Had quite miscarried. I dare be bound again,
           My soul upon the forfeit, that your lord
           Will never more break faith advisedly.

POR.   Then you shall be his surety. Give him this,
           And bid him keep it better than the other.   255

ANT.   Here, Lord Bassanio. Swear to keep this ring.

BASS.   By heaven, it is the same I gave the doctor!

POR.   I had it of him. Pardon me, Bassanio;
           For, by this ring, the doctor lay with me.

NER.   And pardon me, my gentle Gratiano;   260
           For that same scrubbed boy, the doctor's clerk,
           In lieu of this, last night did lie with me.

GRA.   Why, this is like the mending of highways
           In summer, where the ways are fair enough.
           What, are we cuckolds ere we have deserv'd it?   265

POR.   Speak not so grossly. You are all amaz'd.
           Here is a letter, read it at your leisure;
           It comes from Padua from Bellario.
           There you shall find that Portia was the doctor,
           Nerissa there her clerk. Lorenzo here   270
           Shall witness I set forth as soon as you,
           And even but now return'd. I have not yet
           Enter'd my house. Antonio, you are welcome,
           And I have better news in store for you

---

249 *for his wealth* to make him rich.   251 *quite miscarried* been entirely destroyed.   252 *upon* being risked as.   253 *advisedly* deliberately.   254 *surety* guarantee.   262 *In lieu of* in return for.   263-4 *Why, this . . . fair enough* To mend the roads when they are good enough is of course to make the roads bad, since no road is in good condition when it is being mended. Gratiano means that matters were in a better condition as they were before than they are now after the revelation Portia and Nerissa have made [K].   265 *cuckolds* betrayed husbands.   266 *grossly* coarsely, stupidly.   *amaz'd* in a state of complete confusion.   278 *by what strange accident* Portia chooses to make a mystery of the matter, and thus it becomes unnecessary to explain to the audience, who are

Than you expect. Unseal this letter soon.   275
There you shall find three of your argosies
Are richly come to harbour suddenly.
You shall not know by what strange accident
I chanced on this letter.

ANT.   I am dumb.

BASS. Were you the doctor, and I knew you not?   280

GRA. Were you the clerk that is to make me cuckold?

NER. Ay, but the clerk that never means to do it,
Unless he live until he be a man.

BASS. Sweet Doctor, you shall be my bedfellow.
When I am absent, then lie with my wife.   285

ANT. Sweet lady, you have given me life and living;
For here I read for certain that my ships
Are safely come to road.

POR.   How now, Lorenzo?
My clerk hath some good comforts too for you.

NER. Ay, and I'll give them him without a fee.   290
There do I give to you and Jessica,
From the rich Jew, a special deed of gift,
After his death, of all he dies possess'd of.

LOR. Fair ladies, you drop manna in the way
Of starved people.

POR.   It is almost morning,   295
And yet I am sure you are not satisfied
Of these events at full. Let us go in;
And charge us there upon inter'gatories,

---

willing to take it as her whim, but might otherwise wish to know the facts [K].
286 *living* fortune, possessions.   288 *road* anchorage.   295 *starved people*
Lorenzo, though a gentleman, was poor. This accounts for his calling himself an
"unthrift love" in line 16 [K].   296 *satisfied . . . at full* so fully informed about
all these occurrences as to feel no further curiosity [K].   298 *charge . . .
inter'gatories* ask us whatever questions you wish. Interrogatories were formal
questions in writing which witnesses in Elizabethan courts were required (charged)
to answer upon oath. It is appropriate that Portia should use the jargon of the
law courts.

And we will answer all things faithfully.

GRA.   Let it be so. The first inter'gatory   300
That my Nerissa shall be sworn on is,
Whether till the next night she had rather stay,
Or go to bed now, being two hours to day.
But were the day come, I should wish it dark
Till I were couching with the doctor's clerk.   305
Well, while I live I'll fear no other thing
So sore as keeping safe Nerissa's ring.   *Exeunt.*

---

307 *ring* used with a common sexual double meaning.